COLOUR  COLOUR

COLOUR ON COLOUR

JANET HAIGH

PHOTOGRAPHS BY JOHN HESELTINE

SIMPLY STITCHED

⚓ **Anchor**

An Anchor publication

First published in 2004 by
Coats Crafts UK
Lingfield Point
Darlington
Co Durham
DL1 1YQ
UK

Conceived, edited and designed for Coats Crafts UK by
Berry & Co
47 Crewys Road
Childs Hill
London NW2 2AU

Editor Susan Berry
Design Anne Wilson
Technical editor Sally Harding
Illustrations Janet Haigh
Photography John Heseltine
Styling Susan Berry and John Heseltine

British Library Cataloguing-in-Publication Data
A catalogue record for this book is available from the
British Library.

ISBN 1 904485 19 7

Printed in Singapore

CONTENTS

INTRODUCTION

Colour has a direct and personal impact on all of us, whether we recognize it or not. We all have favourite colours – ones that we feel comfortable to wear, to paint our rooms or to choose for planting the flowers in our gardens. Some colours make us feel calm; pale blues, clear watery greens and silvery greys are often chosen to promote soothing feelings, while reds and oranges are supposed to make us feel passionate and excited. We say, "I saw red" when we are describing sudden anger, and we also talk of feeling "blue" when we are sad.

Traditionally, in most cultures, there was a code or symbolism relating to colour, but with the growth of information and interaction now possible between different cultures the meanings are beginning to blur. In Christian-based cultures, for example, blue is for peace, white for purity, red for danger, yellow for jealousy, green for envy. However, in ancient China, yellow, the colour of the sun, was the Emperors' colour and no-one else was allowed to wear it. Royal purple is a colour traditionally worn by western kings and queens, but this is surely a direct descendant of the exclusive use of Tyrean purple for the Roman emperors. This deep purple was made from the shells of crustaceans and so rare and expensive to obtain that it was kept as a special colour for the use of one person – death could result for anyone found wearing the colour as it was seen as an insult to the emperor.

So our attitudes to colour are deeply rooted, both culturally and personally. However, I find that people are nervous of using strong colours, both in their homes and for clothes, unless dictated by fashion. By using colours that you like, even in small proportions, you can really make a difference to your surroundings. Small splashes of colour can make a neutral room look livelier. This book is full of projects that can be made to inject small spots of bright colour into otherwise neutral colour schemes, whether as a cushion or a picture frame, for example. The rich red and pink quilt could be embroidered for a baby, but could just as easily transformed into a blue version if the old adage, "pink for a girl, blue for a boy", holds sway!

The colours in the book are in themselves a personal choice: my own. So even though I am used to dealing with many different colour "stories" and ranges for different design commissions, I still have my own preferences, and people can recognize my work by the choice of colours and the way that I put them together. For instance, I prefer to work with rich pinks rather than strong reds, and generally opt for "in between" colours: purplish blues, yellowy pinks, limy greens, turquoises, violets and mauves.

If, however, you like stronger colours, then you can start to put them together to make vibrant and striking combinations. A good way to start to identify colours that "work" for you is to flick through fashion and interior design magazines or even the pages of this book. Stop at the colours that you like and think about how you might define them. Are they bright or subtle, deep and rich or pale and pretty? Do they look faded or fresh, jewel-bright or softly muted? Get used to identifying the character of the colours that you like and then buy or make small items in them to wear or use in your home.

Easy ways to achieve successful colour co-ordination for your home are to extract the colours for a chosen scheme or accessory from a favourite fabric, a rug or even a bunch of flowers. The embroidered frames on pages 58–61 demonstrate a method of finding colours from any source by using scraps of paper (paint charts are good for this) that match the exact shade of the colours in the scheme. Place the scraps on top of, or next to, the actual colour you are matching. All colours affect other colours, which is why designers and artists work in a white room or studio. Only when colours are seen against pure white or black can their true hue or quality be assessed. Using small bits of fabric and threads to play with in these simple embroidery projects is a quick and easy way to develop your own preferences. The wide range of coloured embroidery threads available makes this craft one of the cheapest and easiest ways of experimenting with colour. Although many of the projects here have recipes for colour combinations, often with alternatives, this book isn't about colour manipulation as such, but rather about trying out new colour combinations.

UNDERSTANDING COLOUR

When designing fabrics I prefer to think in terms of "rainbows" of colour rather than the primary and secondary colour-wheel system so often used to define and describe colour. The rainbow is, in fact, a ribbon of colours that blend into one another, made up of the three primary colours interspersed with the secondary colours; between yellow and red is orange, between yellow and blue is green and between blue and red comes purple. These "between" colours are known as secondary or tertiary colours and they are made by blends of the primary colours (red, yellow and blue), and so called because they are unable to be made from anything but themselves. When you start to mix the secondary or "between" colours together (the tertiary), the really interesting and subtle colours produced are my particular favourites.

A colour harmony is produced easily by choosing one colour – say, red – and then using the colours either side of it in the rainbow, so orange and red and yellow will combine together harmoniously, as will blue and purple and red. Harmonies can be soft or vibrant, and they will never appear to look uneasy or, for that matter, exciting.

If you want excitement, you should try placing opposite colours together – the colours opposite each other in the colour circle (shown left in tapestry wool). In this system, yellow is opposite to purple and orange opposite blue, so, if you put any of these opposing colours together, you will get some vibrant and lively combinations.

Several of the projects have been coloured to blend with another fabric; the bull's-eye cushion colours came from a favourite old Indian silk skirt of mine. But some of the colours have been based on playing with colour harmonies and clashes, almost all starting with the rainbow as a guide.

I hope that the colour combinations and the project ideas in this book give you the confidence to start building your own preferred colour palette, rather than necessarily copying my own, and that they give you the opportunity to start trying out a new range of colours and styles in embroidery. Experiment and have fun!

Getting started

Having the right equipment for any job is essential for good work and any hand sewing will be easier and quicker with the correct needles, scissors and stretchers. At the beginning of each project there is a check list of essential equipment, but it would be useful to assemble a few basic items before you start. The following is an explanation of the purpose they serve, and why you need them.

STITCHING EQUIPMENT

I would suggest that you equip yourself with the following basic items:

You need a box of stainless steel pins and a good range of needles. Buy a packet of assorted sizes of the following needle types: crewel embroidery needles are perfect for most types of embroidery as they have long eyes for ease of threading thicker yarns and sharp points; darning needles are useful for the heaviest threads; "sharps", the ordinary sewing needles with round eyes, can be used for general stitching. If you want to embroider with beads (see project on page 32), then a beading needle is a must. Being shorter, it is easier to manage.

Sharp scissors, in the right size and weight, are essential: two pairs will do to start. A small pair of sharp-pointed embroidery scissors is useful for snipping off threads and for unpicking stitching when things go wrong; a pair of larger dressmaker's shears (medium size) will be needed for cutting out fabrics.

A fine steel thimble, although not essential, is useful if you really do a lot of embroidery. I didn't use one for years, and I still have the scars on the top of my finger to prove it.

You will also need a ruler or tape measure for calculating fabric sizes and cutting out.

Hoops and frames are valuable where the fabric needs to be stretched tight as some embroidery cannot be worked successfully unless the ground fabric is taut. There are various special embroidery frames for this purpose, both round (hoop frames) and rectangular (stretcher frames), which come in a range of sizes. A medium-sized hoop, for working on finer fabric, would be worth including in a basic kit, although many of the projects do not need to be stretched. A small stretcher – the straight-sided version of a hoop – is used for delicate fabrics as a hoop can leave an impression on a finely woven fabric. It is also useful for long strips of fabric that would get in your way if stretched in a hoop (see information on stretching embroidery on pages 90 and 91). I have lots of different sizes of hoops in my workroom, as I think that they are lovely crafted wooden objects in themselves and very inexpensive to buy.

DESIGNING EQUIPMENT

You will also need some basic equipment for creating and transferring designs. A range of graph and tracing papers is useful, depending on the project being undertaken, as is a marker to draw out the design on the fabric to be embroidered. One item of equipment that I cannot do without is a water-soluble pen. Called an Aquatrack marker, it represents the simplest way of getting a design onto the embroidery fabric (see pages 86–7); the blue mark that it leaves can be sponged off with cold water, applied with a cloth or clean paintbrush (provided you remember not to iron the fabric first).

BASIC EQUIPMENT
Here are the basics you will need when starting to embroider – they are all available from Coats. Right (from the top, clockwise): transfer, tracing and graph papers; water-soluble pens and marking pencils; tape measure and ruler; embroidery hoop; stainless steel pins and a selection of different sizes of embroidery and sewing needles; thimble; dressmaker's shears and small embroidery scissors.

Choosing materials

The choice of fabrics and threads can make or mar your work. The following gives you some idea of the range at your disposal, but it is the marrying of the fabric colour, weight and form with the appropriate thread, to suit the style and form of the chosen stitch, that will give your work a truly professional finish. You can, as I do, take your inspiration from a stitched sample and go on to create a project based on this form of embroidery or equally you can have a design idea, and then look for the ideal form of fabric, stitch and thread to work it. Natural fabrics and threads always both look and feel good to work with, and where possible, choose these in preference to synthetics, unless you are looking for a very specific effect – a metallicized yarn for the stitching on shisha mirrors, for example.

FABRICS & THREADS

You can embroider on a wide range of weights and types of fabric, and the type and structure of the weave will determine to some extent the embroidery designs you can employ. I have tried, in this book, to use a range of different fabrics and textures as well as colours, because half of the pleasure in embroidery comes from experimenting with different stitches and varying effects. Those discussed here (and shown on pages 14–15) are just some of the fabrics I like and often use (and have used in this book). It is up to you to discover others!

Materials have been kept as simple as possible: fabrics that will show colours clearly and cleanly, and are easy to use, as this set of designs is aimed at a younger market, with children and teens in mind as well as new home-owners. A whole gamut of colours in all different fabrics, making up rainbows from red through oranges and yellows to greens, turquoises, blues, mauves and purples, back to pinks and reds., embellished with yarns and beads.

Different fabric surfaces can dramatically affect the appearance of colours. Velvets or matte wool cloth will make a colour stronger, or even several shades deeper, depending on the way that the light falls across the surface; a shiny or smooth cloth will make the colour appear lighter and a voile or transparent fabric will render the colour paler and more subtle. Among the plain fabrics are felts, linens, cottons and wools.

Those new to embroidery do not always realize that you can embroider successfully on patterned fabrics as well as plain ones. Indeed, you can use embroidery to enhance an existing design, emphasizing one part of it with particular stitches or decorative embellishment (as in the beaded bag on pages 32–5 and the bolster on pages 52–5). Apart from looking attractive, and very individual, it is a quick and easy way to produce a dramatically different effect. Among the patterned fabrics, ginghams, stripes and informal prints are all easy to source and care for.

For working counted thread stitches, you can purchase canvas or special counted thread (evenweave) fabric (Aida) in a range of colours, and with different gauges. You will also need both backing fabrics (including iron-on adhesive ones) and a variety of lining fabrics, including waddings for quilting.

As far as the threads are concerned, stranded, pearl and soft embroidery cottons have a wide range of uses, while tapestry wools are useful for thicker fabrics and more textured work, and have the advantange that they are quicker to stitch. Space-dyed (Multicolor) yarns in various colours add immediate variety and liveliness to the embroidery. Whether you choose to use toning threads to blend with the colours of the fabric or contrasting ones to emphasize it will depend on the style and nature of the design.

COLOUR, FABRIC AND STITCH

I always sample my designs first to test out stitch types and thread weights and colours, to check their suitability for the design in mind. Here are a few samples I did for the projects in this book so that you can see the range of colours and stitches on some very different fabrics. Samples of the fabrics, threads and embellishments used are shown on pages 14 and 15.

SAMPLES OF MATERIALS

Shown here are some examples of the different weights and colours of fabrics and threads, as well as a few examples of the type of embellishments used for the principal embroideries in this book.

FABRICS

These are a selection of the embroidery fabrics used in this book:

Top left: a range of plain brightly coloured felts suitable for embroidery; top right, patterned cottons in which the pattern can be used for random embroidery; bottom right, medium-weight silk tussah, natural woven linens, raw silk and loosely woven linens inplain colours. In addition to those shown here, you will also need Aida counted thread (evenweave) fabric (for the running-stitch frames on page 58–61), which comes in various colours and gauges. You may also need linings, interlinings, waddings and backing fabrics in various weights and thicknesses.

THREADS

These are a selection of the colours and weights used in this book:

Anchor Tapisserie wool (right); Anchor Pearl Cotton (centre, top); Anchor Soft Embroidery Cotton (right, bottom) and Anchor Stranded Cotton (far right, bottom); Anchor Multicolor (top centre); and metallicized threads, such as Anchor Marlitt (far right).

EMBELLISHMENTS

The following (shown right, centre) are just some of the many different kinds of embellishment for I use for my embroideries:
Beads: silver, clear glass, pearl and iridescent, in shapes including round, rocailles and bugle.
Shisha mirrors: clear, mirrored glass, and mirrors with embroidered edges in a range of colours.
Sequins: Various, in iridescent shades.

GALLERY °F
PROJECTS

PATTERN DARNING

The inspiration for this embroidered flower design is Mexican, where many textiles are made from running stitches worked to look like a woven pattern. The use of variegated or space-dyed yarn, which fades from dark to light to dark along the length of the thread, exploits the quality of this simple embroidery. The colours are very strong in Mexican work as the embroiderers try to capture the vibrant shades of the native flowers. Roses are often worked in a stylistic way but the colours are seldom natural.

Shaded stranded cottons are essential to use for this technique as they will make a flat wide stitch that covers the background easily. The method for preparing the threads is to separate each individual strand of thread from its neighbour before threading the needle, care needs to be taken to align the shading perfectly when reassembling the separated lengths.

I have chosen to work this design on a pair of brightly coloured espadrilles, but you could use it on a bag or purse, or for the corners of a napkin or tablecloth, for example, or on the pocket of a kimono or shirt.

Mexican-style espadrilles

It is great fun to personalize a simple pair of inexpensive espadrilles. You can choose whatever colours take your fancy to make a strong contrast against the fabric colour of the shoes. A flat, darned design like this one uses blocks of colours and creates greater graphic impact. I chose to use bright pinks, greens, blues and yellows on a dark maroon pair for additional contrast, but suggestions for other colour combinations are given on page 23. You could translate the design very easily, if you wished, onto a small bag or purse.

HOW TO MAKE THE DESIGN

The design is embroidered onto the vamps of the shoes and has been carefully worked out so that it is possible to stitch the design in the limited space available. The darning stitches chosen are easy and simple to work, but you need to take care when starting and finishing the design (see instructions on page 22). Variegated threads are ideal for this kind of design, but make sure when selecting them that they have the greatest possible colour variation in the length chosen.

MATERIALS

Pair of brightly coloured espadrilles
One skein each of Anchor Multicolor Stranded Cotton, in five
    bright, contrasting colours
Darning needle
Water-soluble pen
Tracing paper
Transfer paper
Pencil
Scissors
Card cut to fit inside the shoe

EMBROIDERING THE DESIGN

1 Trace the designs from page 108 onto tracing paper, drawing single lines in the stitching gaps. Put a piece of card inside the espadrilles so that you can get a clear tracing of the motif when pressing hard on the back of a contrasting-coloured transfer paper (see page 89 for transfer instructions). Place the lower edge of the motif no more than 6cm (2½in) from the top edge of the espadrille, to allow you to stitch easily inside the vamp.

2 Mark in the guidelines for the stitched areas using a water-soluble pen. Place a line either side of the original drawn transfer line. This double drawn line becomes the gap in the stitching and makes an easy darning guide.

3 Cut a length of thread and separate the six strands before threading the needle, making sure that each length has a good range of variegated colour in it. Put the six strands back together, lining up the shades, then thread the needle.

4 Start stitching from the edges of the design using long straight running stitches (see page 92), voiding the areas between the double blue lines (see instructions on page 22 for starting and finishing).

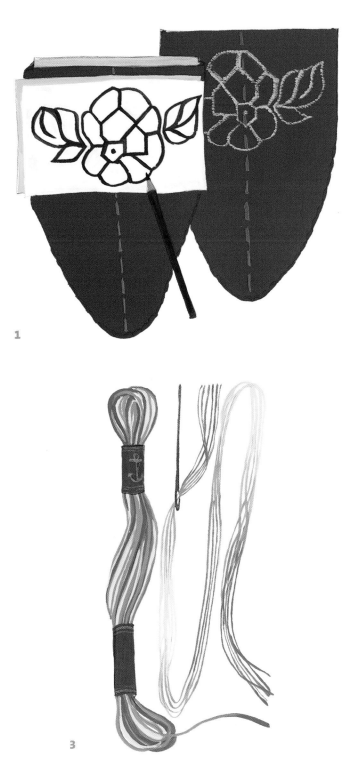

1

2

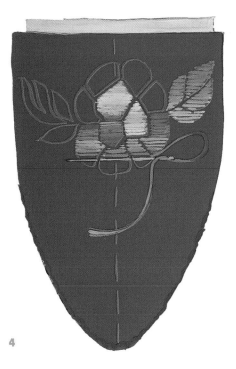

3

4

STARTING & FINISHING TECHNIQUES

1 To start, insert the needle in the middle of the motif leaving a 12mm (½in) tail on top; make a tiny backstitch to secure, then start stitching from the extreme edge of design, so that the stitches cover the thread and hide it.

2 When the motif is completed, pull the thread through to the top of the fabric. Part the stitches and make a tiny backstitch to secure, pull tight and cut – the tail thread should be covered by the rows of stitches.

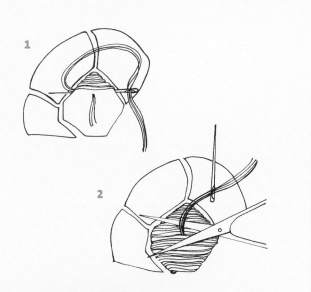

ALTERNATIVE COLOURWAYS

Espadrilles always come in a wide variety of colours and the embroidery can give different effects depending upon the colours chosen. This small motif could also be used to embellish other textiles, but as the stitches are quite long and vulnerable to catching, items that require folding are not really suitable. Whether one or two, or four, colours are used the permutations are so varied that the same motif can look entirely different. Multicoloured thread has been used throughout these alternative colour schemes but if solid colours are used a more graphic effect is produced.

1 This embroidery is in colours that blend with the ground fabric and with one another. There are no sharp contrasts when the mauve, blue and bluish-green threads are stitched onto the purple ground. The way to achieve this effect is to use adjacent colours from the rainbow to that of the background fabric – from purple to indigo blue to turquoise.

2 Just two different shaded threads have been used to stitch this vibrant embroidery. The secret in this case is to stitch the flower in the opposite colour to the ground colour, here a bright pink on a green ground. The leaves and centre have been stitched in the same lime green so that they stand out against the blue-green ground fabric.

3 Here the motif is stitched in another set of three toning shades – red, orange-yellow and green – but they have been placed on a contrasting bright blue ground so that they shine out.

1

2

3

MULTICOLOURED WOOL APPLIQUÉ

The design for this cushion was inspired from the appliquéd woollen penny or button rugs made in the mid-19th century in America and Britain. The scraps of fabric used only needed to be tiny as they were traced around the circumference of small coins or other circular objects; different-sized circles were used so various coins were probably used as templates. The original "pennies" were cut from men's wool suits or old blankets and each was stitched in blanket stitch to reduce fraying before being applied to a single piece of backing cloth with a central cross or star stitch.

In the design on the following pages, I have adapted the idea so that three sizes of "pennies" are embroidered together, using blanket stitch, in a bull's-eye pattern, so that the overall design resembles patchwork. The colours fall into two main groups: brights and neutrals.

If you wish, you could translate the design into other textiles, simply changing the backing fabric. For a cushion, calico is the best choice, for a throw a matching or contrasting wool fabric would look good, backed with the original fabric that inspired the colours perhaps. For a rug, a hard-wearing hessian or canvas backing is essential.

Bull's-eye cushion

The colour scheme for this piece was inspired by a woven striped silk fabric. As felt is available in such a large range of colours and can also be bought in small-sized pieces, it is the ideal fabric for this design. I used a mixture of bright colours with a smaller selection of greys. I also used matching bright colours for the soft cotton threads of the embroidery.

HOW TO MAKE THE CUSHION

Three sizes of "pennies" are embroidered together and then appliquéd onto separate squares of felt, which are applied in turn to abacking fabric, so that the overall design resembles patchwork. You will need to have sufficient bright and neutral colours to make good colour contrasts; play with the colour arrangements until you get a pleasing colour balance. The appliqués are blanket-stitched onto each other, and the whole cushion is then finished with a blanket-stitched edging. The backing fabric is decided by the end use of the piece of appliqué. The cushion measures 48cm (19in) square. When you have embroidered the cushion front, make up the cushion as shown on page 103, and insert the cushion pad.

MATERIALS

Standard felt pieces in 10 colours (5 bright; 5 neutral) to cut 16 of each: small (2cm/¾in); medium 6cm/2¼in); large (10cm/4in)and square (12cm/4¾in)

Felt for cushion back: 2 pieces each 48 x 31cm (19 x 12¼in)

Backing fabric for cushion front, 48cm (19in)

Medium crewel embroidery needle

Anchor *Coton à Broder* no. 16: 3 skeins each of 5 bright colours

Coats monofilament thread

Scissors

Cushion pad, 48cm (19in) square

CREATING THE APPLIQUE

1 Cut out sets of all four templates (see page 109) for the three sizes of circle and the square, from each chosen colour.

2 Arrange the sets of circles and squares together so that the bright and neutral colours alternate, for example, the following sequence of colours demonstrates the combinations: a dark grey small circle on top of a lime medium-sized circle on top of a pale grey large circle on top of a red square. Take some time to play with the colours to achieve pleasing combinations.

3 Start to embroider the sets together by first stitching the small circle to the medium one using a star stitch (see page 98) in a contrasting *coton à broder* thread. Then stitch this, in turn, to the large circle in blanket stitch (see fig 2, page 95) using another contrasting-coloured *coton à broder* thread . Finally, stitch the large circle to the square, again in blanket stitch.

4 Arrange all the completed squares together on the backing fabric, placing the pieces so that a neutral-coloured square is next to a bright one. Pin and baste all the squares in position so that no background shows. Then machine zigzag-stitch the squares to the backing fabric before finally embroidering over the seams in Cretan stitch (see fig 3, page 97), changing the thread colours to contrast with the different patches.

1

2

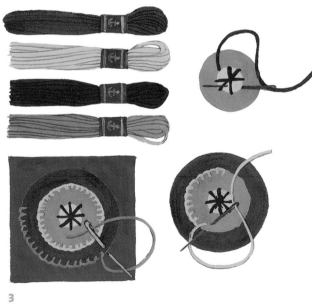

3

4

CHOOSING COLOUR COMBINATIONS

It is possible to create many different looks from the same sets of colours, depending on the proportion of the colours involved. For a completely different look, use just a few of the chosen colours from the range: all the brights or all the neutrals can predominate. The permutations are endless and miraculously the resulting embroideries will still blend with the original fabric that provided the inspiration for the colour palette.

1 In this combination, all the neutrals have been used to make the felt circles and squares, and the bright colours are confined to the embroidery threads. This has resulted in a muted and subtle embroidery that looks both refined and lively at the same time. The felt pieces are still used to create an alternating light and dark design, placed on top of one another and then side by side so that each square contrasts clearly. The brights have been used as embroidery threads so that they clearly stand in a linear design against the softly toned ground.

2 This brilliantly coloured design has omitted the neutral colours altogether, and the brights have been placed one against the other for maximum colour contrasts and clashes – red against pink, backed onto lime green, lime against purple with spots of red and pink. The solid colours dance and vibrate when brilliant turquoise is used as a single colour to embroider everything in position. It would look just as vibrant, and possibly even more dramatic, if one dark neutral was used for the embroidery. Using more than one colour for the embroidery has an overall muting effect, as the eye is distracted by the differently coloured stitches.

1

2

29

BEADED PATTERNS

In folk textiles all over the world, there is a long established tradition of decorating the existing patterns of woven and printed fabrics using embroidery or sequins and beads. In European embroideries the original pattern is sometimes completely covered, but certain Kashmiri shawls were woven with simple designs ready to be embroidered.

The advantage of this technique is that as the colours have already been selected and placed in position it will require less effort to create a strong impression. As a result, it is an enjoyable introduction to stitching and beading. All you have to do is match the colours of the beads to the chosen print. Select a fabric that is basic in its details – blocks of colour or simple well-defined shapes work best, as any subtle shading or linear drawing will be obliterated by the beads. Try not to cover the design completely or it will just look as if you have beaded onto a plain fabric.

In this design for an evening bag, the beading, which is also enhanced by sequins and shisha mirrors, is stitched into position by either stringing the beads on a thread and couching them in position, known as lane or lazy stitch (see page 99), or stitched singly, straight onto the fabric or through a sequin to secure.

Beaded evening bag

This little bag has been beaded and embroidered using a mixture of beads, sequins and shisha mirrors, following the pattern of the fabric. You could limit the extent of the beaded decoration, if you wish, to just a small section in the centre of the bag. The fabric design used here is a simple, multicoloured, irregularly spotted one.

HOW TO MAKE THE BAG

You will first need to enlarge and trace the bag shape (see page 109) and mark out the area to be embroidered on the chosen fabric. Once the embroidery had been completed, you can make up the bag as shown on page 101. You will need to strengthen the fabric to be embroidered with an interfacing, ironed on before you start the embroidery. The bag shown here measures about 21 x 18cm (8½ x 7½in). The bag handles are made from spectacle cords.

MATERIALS

Piece of patterned fabric 30 x 50 cm (12 x 19½in) – the fabric
    used here is Rowan Bubbles design
Iron-on interfacing cut to the same size
Selection of round and straight bugle beads and sequins in
    different sizes, and shisha mirrors with embroidered
    surrounds
Medium-size transparent iridescent sequins
Beading needle
Anchor Stranded Cotton (to match the chosen beads)
Water-soluble pen
Embroidery hoop or straight frame
Pair of spectacle cords (for handles)
Fusible wadding (lightweight) and lining (cut to same size as
    top fabric

BEADING THE BAG

1 Iron on the intefacing onto the wrong side of the patterned fabric. Fold the patterned fabric in half. Using a water-soluble pen, draw the shape of the whole bag onto the right side (see page 106) aligning the base of the bag on the fabric fold line. Mount the fabric on a stretcher of hoop.

2 Slip stitch the shisha mirrors to the centres of the largest spots using self-coloured threads. Sew the sequins to any other medium-sized spots, matching colours as closely as possible.

3 Surround the shishas and sequins and the remaining spots with the smaller beads using different stitching patterns (see page 34). If you wish, you can devise your own stitching patterns instead.

4 Scatter the transparent sequins onto the ground fabric, and stitch them to the fabric using a small bead at the centre of each sequin to secure it. To do this, put the needle through the central hole in each sequin, thread on the bead and return the needle back through the central hole. The bead will then keep the sequin in position. Make up the bag as shown on page 101.

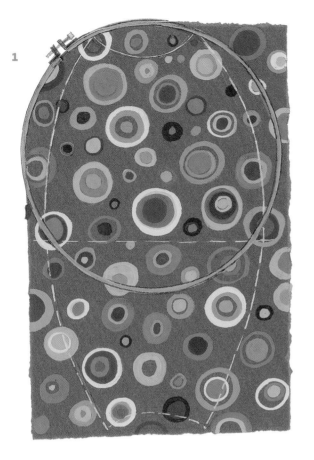

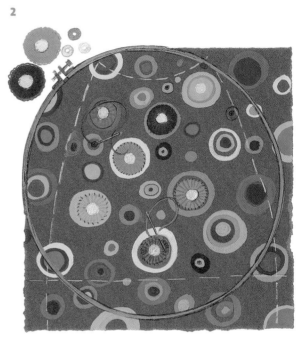

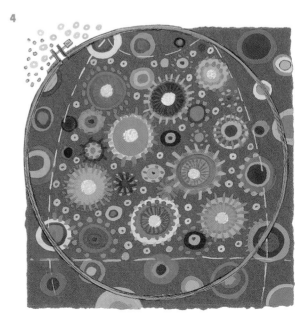

SHISHA VARIATIONS

Here are the different styles of stitching I have used for decorating the beaded bag. You can, of course, create your own designs if you prefer (see page 99 for lazy stitch).

Shisha mirror decorated with row of medium-sized round beads stitched to the edge of the embroidered surround.

Shisha mirror decorated with large round beads placed at intervals around embroidered surround.

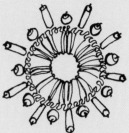

Shisha mirror with alternating bugle and round beads surrounding the embroidered edge.

Central sequin surrounded with small round beads; outer circle sequins secured with tiny beads and interspersed with small beads.

Small round beads stitched directly onto the shisha embroidered surround, with small sequins placed at the perimeter, each secured by a tiny bead added to the stitch through the centre hole.

Central sequin secured with a tiny bead, and a surround of alternating bugles and round beads.

Central sequins surrounded by tiny beads with alternating spokes of bugles and rows of small beads.

Large central sequin secured with small bead and decorated with spokes of different coloured rows of small round beads, stitched on by lazy (lane) stitch.

Large sequin surrounded by spokes of large bugle beads.

BEADED DESIGNS

All types of patterned fabrics can be embellished with beads, sequins or shisha mirrors. The main point to remember is to match the colours to the fabric when selecting the decorative additions. You do not have to create an all-over pattern – the beaded decoration looks most effective when just a few areas of pattern have been selected. .

1 On a striped fabric, the central large stripe is embellished with shisha mirrors, with rows of bugle and round beads decorating adjoining stripes to create a glistening effect.

2 A regularly spotted fabric has been transformed with beaded and shisha decorations, the shisha and starburst bead designs alternating across the fabric in a repeating pattern.

3 A colourful floral fabric has rows of beads that simply follow the patterns of the stems with small decorative groups of beads to enhance the petals. The irregular patterns of the beads turn a basic repeat design into an exclusive "one-off" fabric.

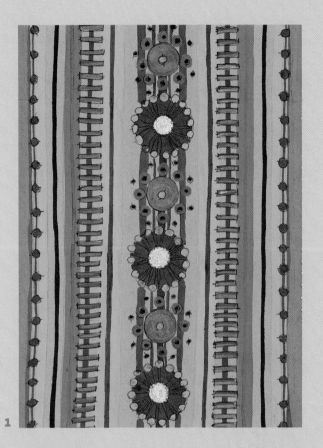

1

2

3

CRAZY PATCHWORK

Crazy patchwork is a form of appliqué that was extremely popular at the end of the 19th century in America and Europe. It is made from a myriad different patterned and plain fabrics overlapping one another in random patterns. The main decorative effect is achieved by embroidering the joins between each patch with different stitches in contrasting threads. In some of the richest pieces, the plain fabric patches are also embellished with embroidery.

The original crazy patchworks were often made from sumptuous fabrics, such as velvets, brocades and silks, instead of the customary hard-wearing cottons and linens, but you can use whatever scraps of fabric you have to hand. For small items, like this album cover, you will only need a limited selection of fabrics. Keep the colour palette to toning colours for a harmonious effect.

Crazy patchwork cover

This design, in toning, differently patterned fabrics, is ideal for covering an album or notebook, but you could very easily turn the same concept into a picture frame (see page 56) or even a cushion cover by enlarging the size of the patches. There is no need to copy the size of the patches too slavishly, as you will be making up the patchwork from scraps of fabric. It is the random nature of crazy patchwork that gives it its charm, but it is probably best to use patches of roughly similar sizes.

HOW TO MAKE THE COVER

This crazy patchwork is worked by first arranging the patches on a backing fabric, then machine stitching them in place, and finally covering the raw edges in a decorative embroidery stitch. The secret to balancing the colours to create a harmonious design is to choose one or two strongly patterned fabrics and to select other plainer ones in colours that match those of the major fabrics. Make sure you have enough fabric in different colours so that you can choose at will. Instructions are given on page 105 for finishing the cover.

MATERIALS

Scraps of colour-co-ordinated fabrics, predominantly Rowan patchwork cottons

Lightweight woven iron-on interfacing: for an A4-size book cover, allow a piece at least 61 x 41 cm (24 x 16in)

Anchor Pearl Cotton no. 5 (in a range of plain and shaded colours similar to the chosen fabrics)

Crewel embroidery needle

Coats monofilament thread

Scissors

Water-soluble pen

Tape measure or ruler

Medium-sized embroidery hoop

Sylko sewing thead

CREATING THE PATCHWORK

1 Lay the book, open flat, on the adhesive side of the iron-on interfacing. With a water-soluble pen draw around the book, then add an extra 5cm (2in) respectively to the top and bottom of the rectangle and 8cm (3in) to the sides (to act as a wrap around). Draw a line at the centre to mark the spine position.

2 Select small pieces of fabrics and place the one with the strongest pattern on the backing fabric, and surround this with a few co-ordinating scraps, cut to overlap one another by about 5mm (¼in). Using a warm iron, press the patches to the interfacing, which should be covered with a sheet of paper to protect any uncovered areas from the adhesive.

3 Continue to assemble the patches in a pleasing pattern to fill in the whole of the surface of the interfacing, overlapping the outside edges a little. Press firmly in place (as in step 2) and then, using monofilament thread, machine zigzag-stitch around the edges of the patches.

4 Stretch the patchwork in an embroidery hoop and work over the seams one at a time with a decorative row of hand-embroidery stitches in a contrasting coloured pearl cotton thread. The stitches can be various but herringbone (see page 96), buttonhole (see page 95) and feather stitch (see page 97) are all traditional. Finally, lightly press with a warm iron.

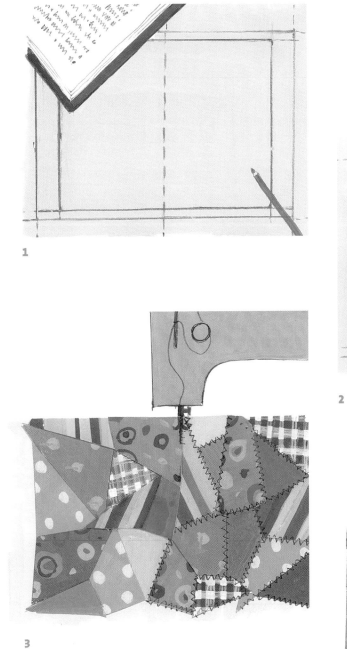

1

2

3

4

HEARTS APPLIQUÉ

Hearts, the universal symbol for love and affection, traditionally embellished children's covers and quilts, whether embroidered, woven or patched. The reds used here, with vibrant pinks and richer shades of plum, symbolize the warmth and protective qualities inherent in this quilt designed for a cot or small child's bed. The narrow strips of fabrics appliquéd with the embroidered hearts could be extended to a larger quilt to make a wonderful wedding gift. The fabrics are all traditional simple cotton prints and plains, embroidered with bold feather stitch in toning red and pink pearl cotton threads. The quilt top is simply padded by tying the backing, padding and surface fabrics together with single knots of multiple embroidery yarns. The hearts are then separately quilted with an outline of tiny running stitches.

Appliqué quilt

Narrow strips of patterned fabric, appliquéd with contrasting hearts in different patterns, make a simple design that works well on a small scale as a cot or child's quilt or on a larger scale as a wedding quilt. Alternating strips of plain and patterned grounds give clarity to a very decorative design. The hearts, whether patterned or plain, have been placed on the ground that gives the strongest contrast. You could translate this design very successfully into a cushion, which would be quicker to make. Use just three rows of hearts for a rectangular cushion.

HOW TO MAKE THE QUILT

This little child's quilt is made with three layers of fabrics – a quilt top, wadding and a backing fabric – which are tied together with single knots of embroidery thread. The heart motifs are applied to the quilt top, stitched in position, and the outlines embroidered in feather stitch. The embroidered top is worked first (shown right), then the quilt is padded and tied. The hearts are separately quilted with an outline of tiny running stitches. The instructions for embroidering the top are given right. Instructions for making up the quilt are given on page 44. This quilt measures 90 x 68cm (35 x 27in).

MATERIALS

5 strips of different ground fabrics, each 70 x 20cm (28 x 8in)
Cotton backing fabric (92cm x 70cm/36in x 28in)
Wadding (92 x 70cm/36 x 28in)
Mixed fabric scraps for heart motifs
Scissors
Fusible web to back 5 strips of ground fabric
Coats monofilament thread
Embroidery hoop
Anchor Multicolor or plain Pearl Cotton no. 5
Medium crewel embroidery needle
Sylko sewing thread
Pins

CREATING THE QUILT TOP

1 Enlarge and copy the heart motif from page 106. Back the fabric scraps for the heart motifs with fusible web and cut out 15 hearts to the size required using the heart template. Place three hearts across each strip of fabric, putting light coloured ones on a dark ground and patterned ones on a plain ground, for example, to achieve the maximum contrast. Bond the hearts into position.

2 Secure the hearts by machine stitching around the edges using zigzag stitch and invisible monofilament thread.

3 Using an embroidery hoop to keep the fabric taut, hand embroider over all the heart outlines in feather stitch (see page 97) in contrasting shades of red and pink pearl cotton (space-dyed threads are ideal).

4 Join all the strips of fabric together, alternating plain with patterned ones. With the right sides together, and using a 1cm (½in) seam allowance, machine stitch the pieces together. Press the seams open and then feather stitch over the seams in toning thread.

1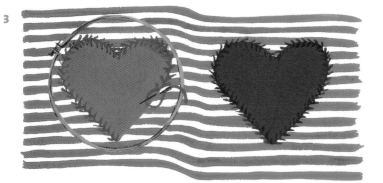

2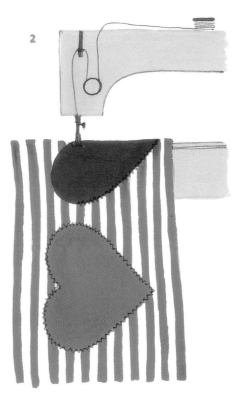

3

4

FINISHING THE QUILT

1 Pin the wadding to the wrong side of the quilt top, and the quilt top to the backing fabric, right sides together. With a 1cm (½in) seam allowance, machine stitch around the edges, leaving a 15cm (6in) gap at one side. Trim the seams and turn the quilt right sides out. Press lightly.

2 Pin the centres of the hearts and then hand-stitch a tiny row of running stitches around the outer edge of each heart using a toning cotton sewing thread. Slip the stitches underneath the decorative feather stitched outline so the quilting is hidden.

3 Make tassels for each heart (see opposite), stitching them to centre of each heart through all the layers of fabric to secure.

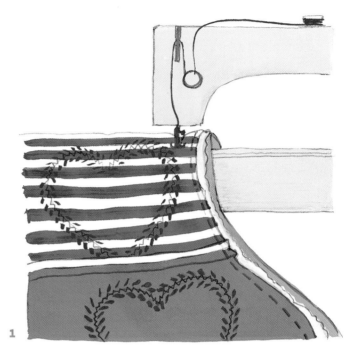

1

2

3

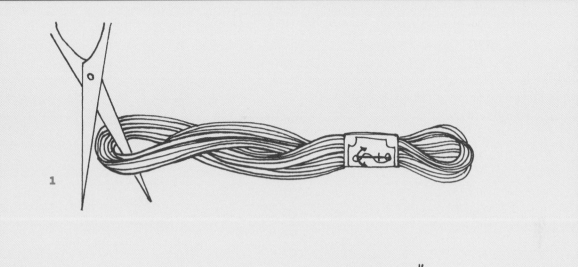

MAKING THE TASSELS

1 Cut four lengths of pearl cotton thread, roughly 1m (1yd) in length, or use four threads of a cut skein of pearl cotton.

2 Fold three times and place in position. With another length of thread in the needle, stitch the strands firmly in place.

3 Form a single knot, around the stitched strands. Cut and neaten the ends to required length.

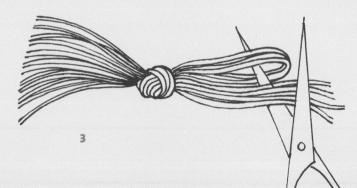

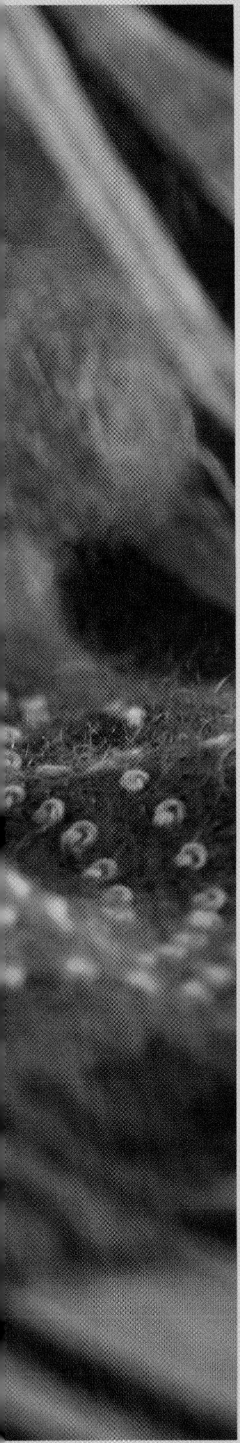

RAISED FRENCH KNOT DESIGNS

Small knots are a very useful textured and decorative stitch found in many countries under different names. In Chinese embroidery there is a decorative technique where entire motifs are stitched in clusters of knots using a slightly flatter variation called Pekin knots.

Small round French knots are most often found in conjunction with candlewicking (see page 51) on early American bedspreads and they are usually white. The raised and precise knots act as a foil to sharpen and detail the more fluffy and softer areas of pattern formed by the candlewicking. However, used on their own they can describe intricate and curvaceous patterns, and they stand out well against brushed and piled fabrics.

The geometric nature of the little knots lends itself to abstract designs like the one shown here – based broadly on an ogee design, made popular in the Renaissance as a symbol for a flower bud – but you could use other simple geometric patterns for this kind of design.

French knot scarf

This fluffy mohair scarf has been given additional textural interest with a simple geometric pattern in French knots, positioned at either end of it. You could, if you prefer, use a plain wool as the ground fabric, but take care that the fabric is appropriate for knotting, which creates some tension on the threads. A similar design, perhaps in toning colours, could be embroidered on a silk evening scarf.

HOW TO MAKE THE SCARF

This scarf measures 36 by 150cm (14 by 60in). You can adapt the pattern to suit the width or size of the scarf (see page 88 for enlarging and reducing designs). This particular scarf is worked in tapestry wool on a mohair ground, but if your scarf is a smooth fine wool or silk, be sure to use an appropriate needle and thread. It is important that the knots sit on the surface of the fabric and do not pull through the weave.

MATERIALS

Wool scarf, either brushed or unbrushed
2 skeins of Anchor Tapisserie (tapestry) wool in a contrasting
    colour for each motif
Medium chenille needle
Water-soluble pen
Embroidery scissors
Tape measure
Straight stretcher frame

EMBROIDERING THE SCARF

1 Trace the design opposite and enlarge it so that it fits within the width of the scarf with at least 4cm (1½in) to spare on either side. Redraw the line of the pattern on your enlargement in a strong colour as you will need to see it clearly through the fabric when transferring it to the scarf. Although this is not difficult if the fabric is loosely woven, if the chosen fabric is a solid wool you will need to use the transferring method on page 89.

2 Place the scarf on top of the design, which should be positioned so that the base of the design is 4cm (1½in) from the bottom edge of scarf. Using a water-soluble pen, draw the outline on the scarf fabric.

3 Stretch the scarf on a straight frame. Then, using tapestry wool, start to stitch French knots (see page 94) along the pattern line, following the contours of the design, so that the reverse stitching appears in neat straight lines. This way the design details will appear the same back and front.

4 It may help to use a tape measure to stitch the first row or so of stitches as the knots need to be uniformly spaced, about 1cm (½in) apart. As you get used to the rhythm of the stitch, or if you are already an experienced embroiderer, you can dispense with the tape measure.

1

2

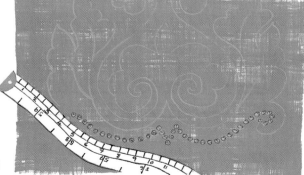

3

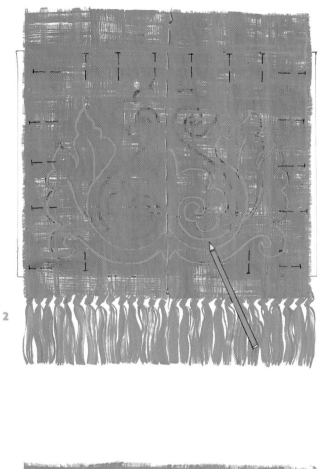

4

C A N D L E W I C K

Traditional candlewick decoration was worked with both unbleached calico and cotton yarn that is similar in appearance and thickness to the wick at the centre of a candle, hence the name. The original designs, which involved looped stitches that were then cut to create a raised pile, incorporated many different patterns and stitches and were used for beautiful bedspreads and carpets. The technique relied on washing the finished piece to fluff out the pile: the fabric would shrink when washed, trapping the cut loops securely in the ground fabric.

Brightly coloured candlewick designs look best when bold, and lines and spots are relatively easy to work. The simple stitches I use are worked with multiple strands of yarn that fluff up to at least three times their initial size after washing. However, if you use modern pre-shrunk fabrics, then an iron-on fusible backing fabric will be needed behind the embroidered areas to prevent the loops from being pulled through.

The effect of the technique on a coloured ground is to enrich and darken it slightly, so choose a lighter shade of thread when matching the threads to the background colours.

Candlewick bolster

I have created a large bolster, ideal for a garden sofa for example, on a striped ground, using the stripes to dictate the candlewicking colours and patterns. You could just as easily turn this into a smaller bolster, or rectangular cushion, if you wish.

HOW TO MAKE THE BOLSTER

The bolster here is made in three pieces – a centre piece and two end pieces – and measures 25cm (10in) in diameter and 90cm (36in) long. After working the embroidery, you then assemble the bolster, and add the cords and tassels at each end (see page 104 for making up instructions).

When estimating threads for a bolster, a skein of Anchor Soft Embroidery Cotton makes a 50cm (18in) line of tufting; a 5cm (2in) spot takes about 1½ skeins. You will need a very large darning needle for this technique, as the eye must be big enough to enable the double quantity of thread to pass easily through the fabric. If the fabric has been pre-shrunk you will need a couple of pieces of iron-on interfacing the same size as the embroidered area of the bolster.

MATERIALS

1.8m (2yd) striped fabric (112cm/44in wide)
Anchor Soft Embroidery Cotton in colours to match the stripes
Very large-eyed darning needle
Water-soluble pen
Small embroidery scissors
Dressmaker's shears
Embroidery hoop or large straight stretcher frame
Iron-on interfacing for backing embroidered areas
Anchor Soft Embroidery Cotton in suitable colour for cords and
    tassels
Bolster to fit

EMBROIDERING THE BOLSTER

1 Mark the lines of stripes and spots at each end of the large central piece of fabric (see page 104). Draw the lines either side of the spots so that they are different colours and use all the colours in the stripes.

2 Stretch the fabric on a hoop or frame. Using soft cotton embroidery, work the spots first. Form them by stitching small spirals in spaced-apart backstitch (see page 98), leaving loops of around 2cm (¾in) on the surface of the embroidery as you make each stitch. Pull the loops often as you work to ensure they are even in length. Cut all the loops in one spot before moving to the next one.

3 Work the tufted stripes on a stretcher or, if the hoop won't go over the worked spots, embroider them while holding in your hands – they are fairly quick and easy to do. Work the tufting as for the spots, but this time make the spaced backstitches in a straight line. Cut through all the loops as you finish each line. When you have completed the four rows of stripes and one row of spots at one end, work the other end of the bolster similarly.

4 Iron the pieces of interfacing on the back of the embroidered areas and wash the fabric in hot water. Once it is dry and the cut loops have fluffed up, trim them carefully to an even height using embroidery scissors. Then finish the bolster (see page 104) and the drawstring and tassels (see pages 54 and 55).

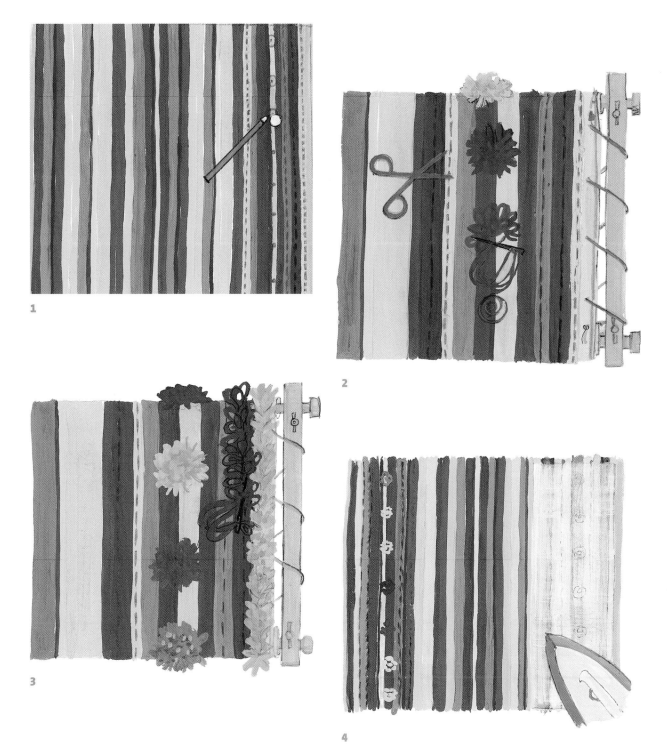

1

2

3

4

MAKING A CORD

The instructions here are for a two-toned cord.

You will need roughly 2.5m (3yd) of soft embroidery cotton in two colours to make the bolster cords as the threads should be at least two and a half times longer than the required length of the finished cord. You will need a hook fixed securely into a board (or alternatively use a window catch or door handle, or indeed anything that will give you a secure purchase).

1 Tie the first thread into a loop and place over a hook. Place a pencil in one end of the loop and twist clockwise until the thread forms a tightly twisted cord – the longer it needs to be, the more twists required. Maintain a tight tension on the threads as you work.

2 Take the second thread and twist it exactly the same number of times in the same direction.

3 Place the two (or more) threads together and now twist together in the opposite direction, at least 15 times. When the thread starts to twist in on itself it is tight enough. Cut off the knotted ends.

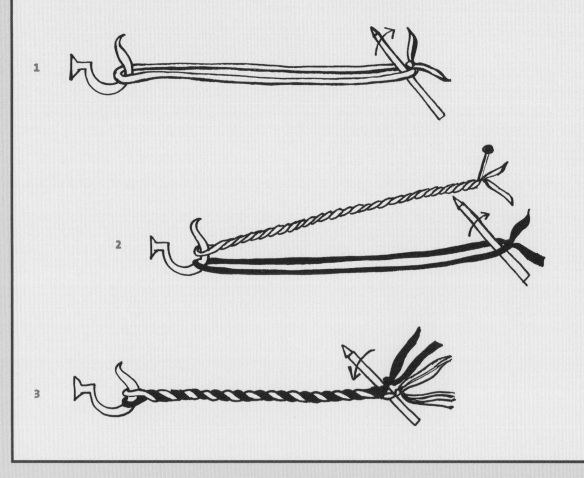

MAKING BOLSTER TASSELS

Tassels are an attractive form of decoration. An easy way to make a tassel, if it is wool, *coton à broder* or stranded cotton, is to use the whole skein. If it is pearl cotton, you will need to remove the bands and fold the skein in half before proceeding as follows:

1 Remove the lower band and cut through all the threads at that end of the skein.

2 Make a loop through all the tops of the threads to secure the tassel. Select a long length of self-coloured thread and make a loop in one end, leaving a length of thread longer than the finished tassel.

3 Whip the other end around the top of the threads in a neat spiral covering, and secure the loop. Thread the end of the whipping yarn through the loop and pull it so that the loop disappears under the whipping.

4 Thread the top end of the whipping yarn in a large needle and feed this into the middle of the tassel. Trim the ends to level them.

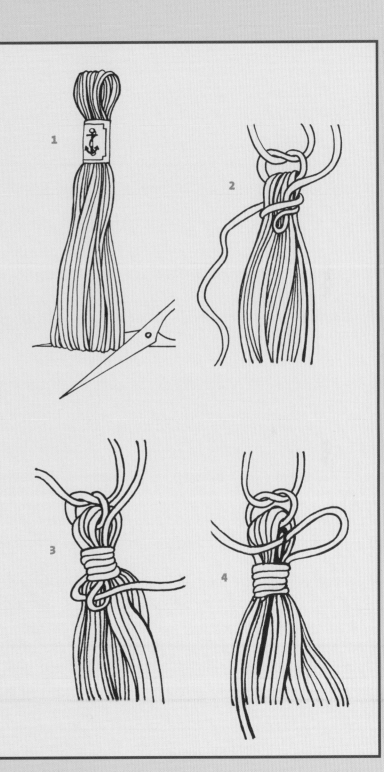

RUNNING-STITCH EMBROIDERY

Running stitch is the simplest and probably oldest stitch of all. Used as both a regular sewing stitch for basting fabrics together, prior to machine or hand stitching, it also is one of the most popular embroidery stitches. It is the basic stitch for quilting fabrics together in a variety of designs and motifs and it is also used for darning, where it forms patterns of zigzags, diamonds or crosses from rows of carefully counted thread stitching.

Here it is also used for a counted-thread design, a straight line of perfectly uniform and evenly spaced stitches. The key to this accurate spacing is the fabric that it is stitched onto: Aida is an evenweave fabric designed specially for counted-thread embroidery, particularly for cross stitch. Most evenweave fabrics are meant to be covered completely but Aida is designed to be seen and comes in a wide range of colours. Like canvases, it is available in different counts of 11, 14, 16 and 18 stitches to an inch. Used here for picture frames the fabric ensures that the stitches will be perfectly spaced in a smart and graphic pattern.

Running-stitch frames

Simple graphic embroidery designs and stitches are ideally suited to picture frames, as their linear quality does not distract the eye from the central image. It is a good idea when choosing colourways for the frame to use the colour or style of the central image to direct your choice. In these two little frames, I have chosen a black ground with contrasting, brightly coloured stitches for the black and white picture of the dog, and a bright red ground with colours that tone with the little flower picture.

HOW TO MAKE THE FRAME

You will need to either use a bought frame kit or make your own little cardboard frame, over which the fabric for the embroidery is stretched. Aida fabric is ideal for the ground fabric, as you can use the evenweave threads to ensure your stitches are all of an even length. Using a separate needle for each colour saves time as you do not have to rethread the needle for each new colour. The running stitches used are shown on page 92. Once you have completed the embroidery, you will need to make up the picture frame itself (see page 102).

MATERIALS

Cardboard frame kit or a piece of cardboard cut to correct
    format and size
Black 11-count Aida fabric, 5cm (2½in) larger all around than the
    chosen frame
Anchor Soft Embroidery Cotton: one skein each of red (46), pink
    (27), purple (98), blue (131), green (241), yellow (295) and
    orange (303)
Wadding (same size as frame)
Fabric glue
Several medium-sized tapestry needles
Embroidery scissors
Silver marking pencil

EMBROIDERING THE DESIGN

1 Choose the thread colours to match the image you are proposing to frame, and which will contrast well with the chosen ground fabric (see page 60).

2 Lay the cardboard frame face down on the Aida fabric and draw round the outer and inner edges using the silver marking pencil. It is easier to draw along the lines of holes to get an even line. Draw four lines at right angles from each corner of the inner rectangle to create a brick pattern. Make sure that the same number of holes is counted for each section of the frame to ensure even stitching over the whole frame.

3 Start stitching along the first line in red, making a small backstitch, rather than a knot, to secure (knots create bumps when the frame is made up). Stitch over three threads of ground fabric, under one thread, and over three threads to create the pattern. Continue to the end of the row, fastening off with another backstitch outside the frame edges. Stitch the second colour on the next row next to the first, leaving a set of threads in between. Work the rest of the colours, as shown, to complete the first side of the frame.

4 Start the next side of the frame, missing one set of threads and then working the first row in red. Repeat the colours (as for the first side) to the end of this side of the frame. Continue to space all the rows identically (with such a uniform design any mistake will be all too obvious when see it from a distance).

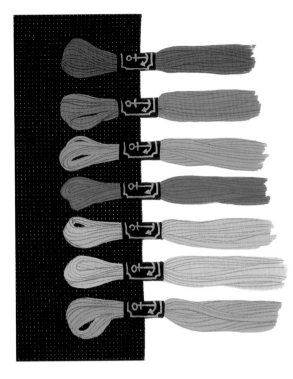

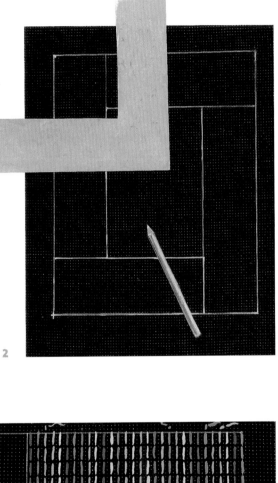

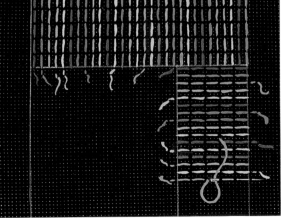

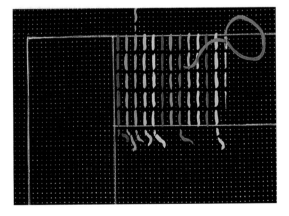

DESIGNING FRAME EMBROIDERIES

If you colour match the frame to the picture that it surrounds, even a detail of a postcard will look really special. If you make the frame quite a bit larger than the picture, the central image gains importance. For a square picture, cut a small square paper frame and place it over the area of the picture that you wish to frame. Tape this in position at the back and take it with you when you select the thread colours. Decide on the colour of the Aida ground, which will be the dominant colour of the frame. Match the yarns to the other colours in the central image by holding the threads close to it. Look really carefully at the colours as they are often different from what you would expect – the star shape in the image below looks white, but when you compare it to a white thread, it is, in fact, a creamy peach colour; white would stand out too strongly if placed in the rows of stitches.

For the frame below, I chose two pinks to match the flowers, two purples for the vase, two greens – one soft and one brighter – for the leaves and stalks and two blues from the centres of the flowers. Set all the threads against the picture with the ground colour and reject or replace any colours that jump out. In the frame, opposite, a simple set of contrasting colours was used.

The stitching instructions on the previous page can be adapted to suit the frame shape and size. For example, a smaller frame might need smaller, more closely spaced stitches.

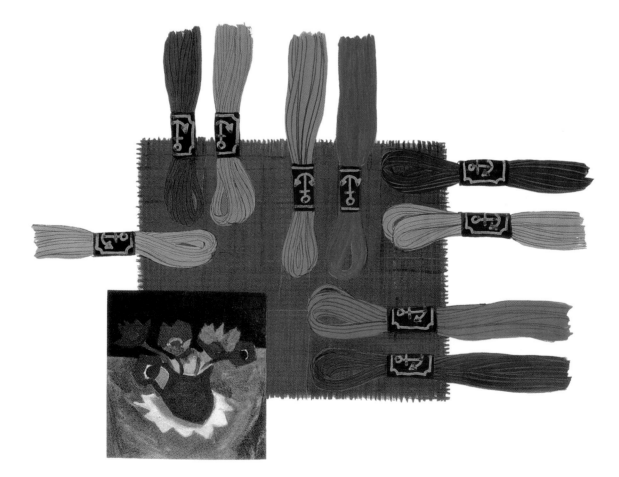

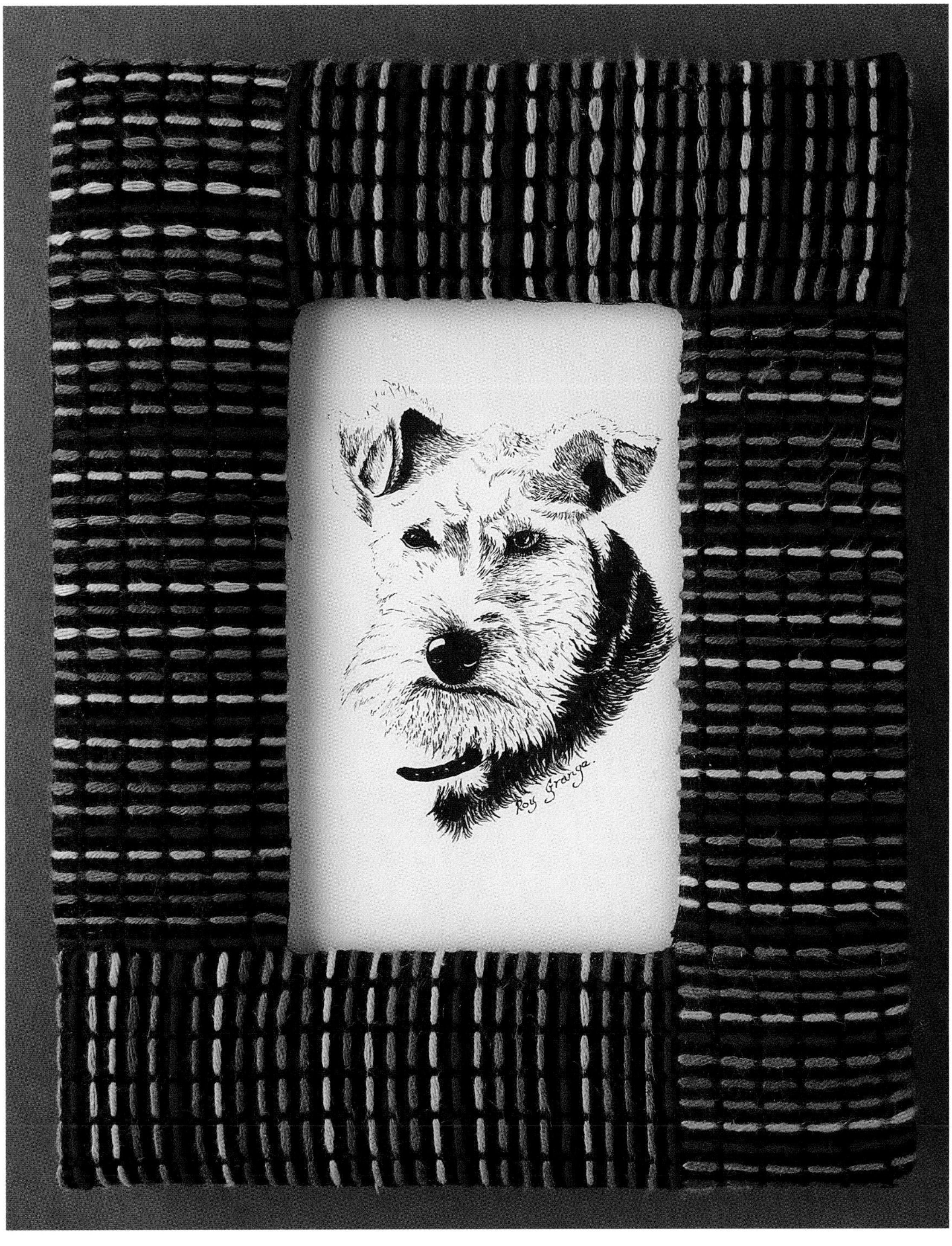
Roy Grange.

PICTORIAL MOTIFS

This rose and bow motif was inspired by the embroidered household linen so popular throughout Europe in the 19th and early 20th century. Most girls were taught to stitch at an early age and these motifs can also be found on European samplers of the same era, but on a much smaller scale.

In Germany and Switzerland particularly, romantic pictures of flowers, garlands, bows and birds were stitched in fine linear designs on cushion covers, tray cloths and pillows, and on bags used to carry home the freshly baked bread from the local baker. All kinds of images adorn this style of embroidery, including children dressed in costumes, complete with clogs and neckerchiefs, set against windmills, and even household objects are employed, such as tea and coffee cups and pots – even sewing machines are depicted! The original embroideries were stitched in red or blue on white linen and are very elegant and crisp in appearance. The simple embroidered line used for the drawing is always subtle in its undulations: stem stitch is often used for the linear elements and satin stitch for the larger areas, to create an expressive and rhythmical motif.

Traditional floral motif

Here a favourite linen shirt has been given a new lease of life with a bright and contrasting-coloured embroidery that decorates the pocket area. You could use the motif on a shirt or blouse, a dressing gown or kimono, or even on the pocket of a pair of jeans.

HOW TO MAKE THE MOTIF

You will need to first transfer the design to the chosen garment, enlarging the motif on page 108. It pays to pick out brightly contrasting colours when embroidering onto vividly coloured garments, but a toning motif can look good on deeper coloured fabrics – for example on a pair of jeans. If you are embroidering onto or over a pocket, slip a piece of card into it first, to make sure you do not stitch through the layers of the fabric. Before stitching fine fabric, to ensure it does not buckle, you should bond an iron-on interfacing to the embroidery ground, and stretch the area to be worked in a small hoop.

MATERIALS

Coloured linen or cotton garment, with or without a pocket
One skein of Anchor Pearl Cotton no. 5 for each colour (here, two red and pink threads and two contrasting colours in bright green and turquoise)
Medium-sized embroidery hoop
Medium crewel embroidery needle
Iron-on backing fabric (slightly larger than the motif)
Dressmaker's carbon paper
Water-soluble pen
Small embroidery scissors

EMBROIDERING THE DESIGN

1 Trace the motif, from page 108 and enlarge it to the size required. Press the interlining onto the back of the shirt front. Lay the shirt on a flat surface and place a piece of dressmaker's carbon paper over area to be embroidered. Lay the motif design on top and, pressing very hard, transfer the design onto the fabric, drawing over any pocket as well.

2 Reinforce the drawing using a water-soluble pen and if there is a pocket, draw a little extra stem inside it so that the pattern will be continuous even when the pocket gapes.

3 Place the hoop over the bow and stem section of the design, and, if this is on top of the pocket, place the card inside it before starting to stitch. Thread the needle with the pink thread and stitch one whole bow outline in stem and satin stitch (see page 94), then fill the rest of the outline with the red thread in satin stitch. Next, stitch the stem (one side in lime and one side in turquoise), carefully finishing off the thread inside the pocket by running it between the top fold of material.

4 Move the hoop to the top section of the design and embroider the rose, the inside swirl and enfolding petal in red and the outside petals in pink in stem and satin stitch. Stitch the leaves in a mixture of green and turquoise thread, using the illustration, right, as a guide. Finally stitch the stem, extending the stitching into the pocket if needed. Sponge off the pen marks and press with a steam iron on the inside.

ALTERNATIVE DESIGN COLOURWAYS

These three alternative rose embroideries are worked to the same colour principle as the shirt – that of working the motif in contrasting colours to the background. The theory behind this is shown in the introduction on pages 14 and 15 where the wools have been spread out to form a circular rainbow or colour wheel. Opposite colours on the wheel contrast, so you will see that red and green are contrasts, as are orange and blue or yellow and violet. When these colour combinations are used together the effect is always strong and bright, and sometimes so dazzling that the colours appear to vibrate. Solid, as opposed to shaded, coloured threads have been used for the embroidered shirt to create a stronger contrast. If, however, you want a softer and more relaxed look to your embroidery, work these colours on a toning coloured ground (picking a colour nearest to it on the colour wheel – for example, the reds and pinks could be embroidered on a soft mauve ground or the golden yellows and oranges embroidered on a cream ground.

On a blue ground the rose motif is embroidered in contrasting colours of golden yellow and orange, with the leaves worked in two shades of green. The warm tones of these colours look fresh and vibrant against the rich deep-blue ground fabric. The colours in this motif would look even more brilliant on a bright turquoise ground.

In this combination the violet and purples of the flower and bow are worked on a bright orange-yellow ground fabric. Can you believe that the green used for the leaves in this colourway is exactly the same colour as the one in the other two alternative designs? From this, you can see just how colours behave when placed on contrasting coloured, as opposed to complementary coloured, grounds.

This hot magenta ground fabric has a lime green and citrus yellow embroidery as its contrast, while the same greens as before – a bluish-green and sap green – are used for the leaves and stalks.

FLAME-STITCH CANVASWORK

Flame stitch, Florentine or Bargello are the popular names for this type of straight-stitched canvas embroidery. Variations of this technique, which relies purely on colour for its effect, are found throughout Europe and America. It is most commonly used for covering household articles, as it is extremely hard-wearing. Chair seats, cushion covers, firescreens and even rugs have been worked using this distinctive pattern. It normally relies for its effect on using tones of quite subtle colours, but I have broken with tradition by using different fresh and bright colours that all have similar tonal values and repeating the whole sequence of the design over the entire canvas, rather than opting for a small, repetitive pattern.

The technique is very simple and relies on counting either the threads or holes of the background canvas to ensure a perfect patterned result. Each straight stitch is made over several threads – in this case over seven at a time. I chose the largest number advisable for the canvas count and the thickness of the wool to make it as quick to stitch as possible.

Flame-stitch cushion

This small rectangular cushion would look good as the centrepiece of a collection of cushions in toning colours. However, if you wanted to turn the design into a stool cover, for example, it would be possible to extend the design both horizontally and vertically to fit any rectangular shape. As the pattern is worked over seven threads of medium-gauge counted canvas, it is relatively quick to do.

HOW TO MAKE THE CUSHION

This cushion is easy to work. It measures 40 x 28cm (16 x 11in) when finished. One colour is put in at a time across the whole canvas and then each subsequent colour is placed in exactly the same formation above and below it, creating a wave-like effect across the canvas. The chart for the cushion is on page 108 and indicates a single line of colour only. You will need a piece of canvas roughly 2cm (¾in) larger all around than the proposed cushion. Once the embroidery is completed, make up the cushion as shown on page 103.

Finally, make four tassels (see page 55) out of four different colours. Stitch each one to each corner using the same coloured threads.

MATERIALS

Piece of 12-count canvas ,44 x 32cm (17½in x 12½in)

2 skeins each Anchor Tapisserie (tapestry) wool: orange (8140), purple (8588), pink (8524), green (8986), lime (9274), yellow (9284), green-blue (8918)

One additional skein each of four of these colours for the tassels

Medium tapestry needle

Water soluble pen

Embroidery scissors

Masking tape

Backing fabric, 2 pieces each 31 x 32 cm (12¼ x 12½in)

Sylko sewing thread

Cushion pad, 40 x 28cm (16 x 11in)

EMBROIDERING THE CUSHION

1 Having cut the canvas to size, stick the masking tape over the raw edges. of the canvas to protect your hands and wrists from getting scratched and to stop the edges of the canvas from unravelling. Using a water-soluble pen, mark a right angle 2cm (¾in) in from the lower left-hand corner as a guide for the edge of the design.

2 Turn to page 108 for the chart. Using the purple thread, start stitching the design at the bottom left-hand corner. Knots are not used in canvaswork, so insert the needle from the back of the canvas, through the corner hole. Leave a small length of thread at the back and hold it into position, trapping it with the subsequent stitches. Count six threads and return the needle through the next hole, so that each stitch covers seven canvas holes. Follow the chart all the way to the top right-hand corner – the length of the stitch never changes, only the placement. When the first colour is completed to within 2cm (¾in) from the edge of the canvas, draw the rest of the outline around the canvas, 2cm (¾in) from the edge.

3 Stitch the second colour in the sequence above the first.

4 When the whole sequence of seven colours has been completed start again with the first colour. When the embroidery is completed, steam press lightly on the back – there should not be any warping of the canvas as the stitches are straight.

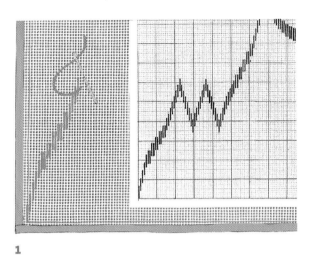

1

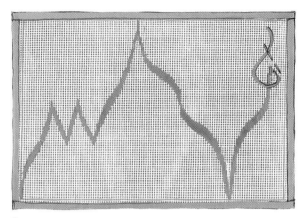

2

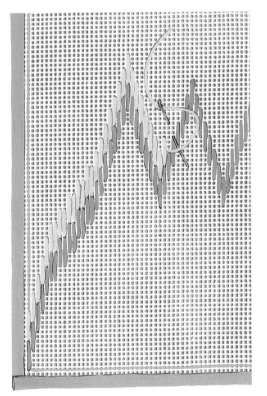

3

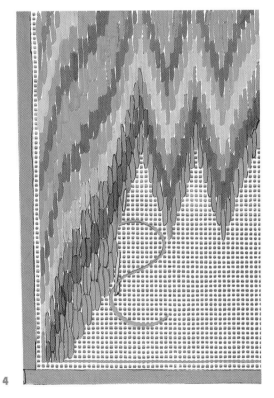

4

ALTERNATIVE DESIGNS AND COLOURWAYS

In traditional Bargello patterns the colours are muted and follow one another in shaded variations. The colours I have chosen produce a strong and large pattern overall. There are many variations using the set of colours I have chosen here. You will find that all the colours except the lime have both lighter and darker shades in the Anchor tapestry wool range and many different effects can be achieved by playing with the colour placement. Sample several versions on a spare piece of canvas to get the look that you want. The resulting designs could be made up into other projects in the book, such as the larger of the two bags (see page 76) or the book cover (see page 38).

1 In this example, the same set of colours are stitched in a more traditional system with the colours following one another closely like a gradated rainbow. This causes the width of the zigzag to appear broader. Seen up close, it looks quite subtle but when viewed from a distance it becomes a very strong pattern.

2 In this example, two colours have been chosen from the initial group – the pink and green – to which lighter and darker have been added to form a graduated striped zigzag effect.

3 In this example, all the colours have been used in a random pattern so that every potential colour combination can be enjoyed. This would be a good starter for someone who just likes to use colour as they can stitch any they like together to form lively and contrasting patterns.

1

FELT FLOWERS

Felt is probably the oldest man-made fabric, consisting of layers of wool matted by water and heat into a continuous, solid sheet. As it is not woven, it does not fray when cut and this makes it very easy to work. Felt has been used as a basis for embroidered wool rugs in India and for appliquéd blankets in the Balkans, and it has always been popular as a material on which children learn to stitch because it is so easy to cut and sew.

Felt is now mostly made from synthetic materials and is usually easily obtained in a wide range of bright colours. Modern felt-makers experiment by embedding different materials into the felt, but the design shown on these pages emphasizes the beauty of the matte finish, using a harmonious choice of colours.

The three-dimensional felt flowers depcited were very popular during the latter years of the 19th century, and in the early 20th century. They were usually wired up into small bunches to wear as a corsage or as single flowers to decorate a hat. Here a few flowerheads have been arranged above a vase or basket shape against a pieced felt ground. The design could be used to decorate many different items, from a tea cosy or cushion cover to a book cover or a bag.

Felt-flower bag

This retro-style design has been used for a simple fabric shopping bag. You can make up the design and apply it to a shop-bought bag, or you can use the design for cushion cover, for example. The choice of toning colours helps to pull the design together, but you can opt for a similar blend in, say, mauves, blues, greys and pinks.

HOW TO MAKE THE BAG

You will need felt pieces in five toning colours. The bag shown here measures 37cm (15in) square, so the two main colours (turquoise and mauve) need to be bought to fit the width of the chosen bag. You can make up the design on a piece of ground fabric and then simply oversew it neatly onto the chosen bag. To make a cushion, see page 103.

MATERIALS

Turquoise felt, 40cm x 21cm (16 x 8in); mauve felt, 40 x 15cm
    (16 x 5½in)

Small pieces of felt in the other colours

0.5m (½yd) backing canvas

2 skeins of Anchor Soft Embroidery Cotton in colours to match
    the main fabric

Medium crewel embroidery needle

Water-soluble pen

Scissors

Pins

Sylko sewing thread

STITCHING THE EMBROIDERY

1 Place the pieces of turquoise and mauve felt on the ground fabric, and pin and baste in position. Using the pattern for the basket on page 107, cut out the basket shape and pin in position on the centre of the background, aligning the seam allowances. Using soft cotton, embroider the herringbone stitch (see page 96) between the two background colours and work Jacobean trellis stitch (see page 99) onto the basket.

2 Using the patterns on page 107, cut out the leaves and small circles and assemble the 3D flowers (as shown on pages 78–9).

3 Arrange the flowers in position on the ground, pin and baste a circle of felt in the middle and work a star stitch (see page 98) in soft cotton at the centre of each flower to secure it. On the petalled flowers work a French knot (see page 94) in the centre of each petal so that they won't droop too much when used. Catch the backs of the folded-petal flowers with a few stitches in a toning sewing thread.

4 Position the small dots of felt between the large flowers and work star stitches to secure them. Stitch the leaves in position with a matching soft cotton thread using running stitch (see page 92).

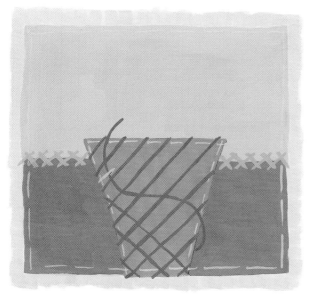

1

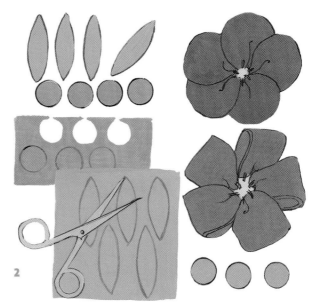

2

3

4

MAKING FOLDED-PETAL FLOWERS

1 Using the patterns on page 107, cut five pieces of felt measuring 7 x 3cm (2¾in x 1¼in) plus one small 2-cm (¾-in) square. Cut one central disc 2cm (¾in) in diameter in another colour.

2 Fold each rectangle of felt in half and trim off the corners for the petals.

3 Stitch the folded petals to the small square with a few straight stitches in a matching coloured thread, overlapping the edges of the petals.

4 Make a little tuck at the left-hand bottom edge of each petal so that it folds softly over the adjoining petal.

5 Place the flower on the embroidery, position the central circle and, using a soft embroidery cotton, stitch through all the layers in star stitch (see page 98).

MAKING ROUND-PETAL FLOWERS

1 Using the patterns on page 107, cut five petal shapes, plus a small square and a central disc.

2 Make a small tuck in the centre of the base of each petal and secure with a few straight stitches in a matching thread.

3 Sew the petals to the small square of felt, overlapping each one on the left-hand side. Finish as for step 5 of the folded-petal flower.

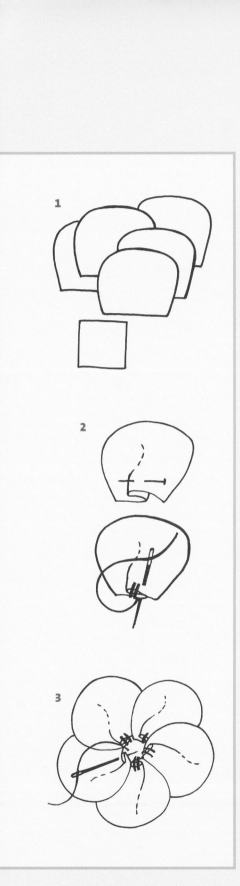

SHISHA MIRRORS

The shisha mirrors and sequins used in this little hat traditionally decorate children's hats and garments in southern India. Mirrors and shiny sequins are featured on many tribal embroideries as the sun glinting on the surface dazzles the eyes and this is thought to deflect the "evil eye" away from whoever is wearing the garment, so precious children are doubly protected by little hats like this one.

There are many ways in which the little pre-embroidered mirrors now available can be further embellished, but they are easily stitched into position with a few hidden slip stitches. Traditional Indian embroidery features many round stitching patterns for working in conjunction with the mirrors. These are always executed in brilliant colours and sometimes tiny metal sequins that further reflect and refract the light are stitched between the mirrors.

I have designed a little hat and belt in this style, but you could choose to apply the mirrors, if you prefer, to a small round cushion or perhaps the cuff or hem of a garment.

Shisha-mirror hat

The design for this little hat is very simple to make – just a circle of fabric for the crown with another length of fabric stitched to it. If you prefer, you can make an even easier alternative – the decorated belt shown on page 85. The pre-embroidered mirrors and sequins come in a wide range of colours, but will look most attractive when the ground fabric tones and the mirrors are in the same tonal range.

HOW TO MAKE THE HAT

You will need first to cut out the hat base from felt. You then embroider the crown and sides of the hat with the mirrors before stitching the hat pieces together. Follow the steps, right, to embroider the hat, and then the making up instructions for the hat itself on page 84. The diameter of the hat measures 19cm (7½in). One size fits all as there is a small vent at the back.

MATERIALS

1 piece of felt approx 30 x 60 cm (12 x 24in)
1 piece of felt for hat lining in contrasting colour
Iron-on medium-weight interfacing fabric for hat band,
    6 x 56cm (2½ x 22in)
30 pre-embroidered shisha mirrors in four different
    colours: pale blue, peach, mauve and lime green
1 packet of silver sequins
2 skeins each of Anchor Marlitt in pale blue (1009), peach
    (1044), mauve (816) and lime (1029)
1 skein Anchor Marlitt in lime green (1029) for stitching
    the borders
Small crewel embroidery needle
Small "sharp" needle, for the sequins
Water-soluble pen
Embroidery hoop (optional)

EMBROIDERING THE HAT

1 On the chosen felt, mark out and cut the patterns (see page 109) for the hat band and crown, leaving a good allowance around the edges if you want to use an embroidery hoop. (You may have to cut the hat band in sections if you are using small pieces of felt, so allow an additional 1cm/½in for each seam.) With a water-soluble pen, mark out the circles shown on the patterns.

2 Apply the first mirror to the centre of the crown by slip stitching it with one strand of matching Marlitt thread. Using all six strands of thread, embroider the larger circle pattern using the pen line as a guide (see fig 5, page 97).

3 Pin the next ring of mirrors into position, using the other chosen colours, and embroider them alternating three large circle designs with three small ones (see fig 4, page 97). When completed, put in the last circle of mirrors using all the colours and alternating the circle sizes as before. Scatter the sequins in any gaps between the embroidery, sewing them on using a French knot and three strands of matching Marlitt thread (see page 94).

4 Embroider the band of the hat in the same way using all the colours and scattering the sequins in any gaps. Press lightly on the backs of the embroideries using a low temperature. The hat is now ready to be made.

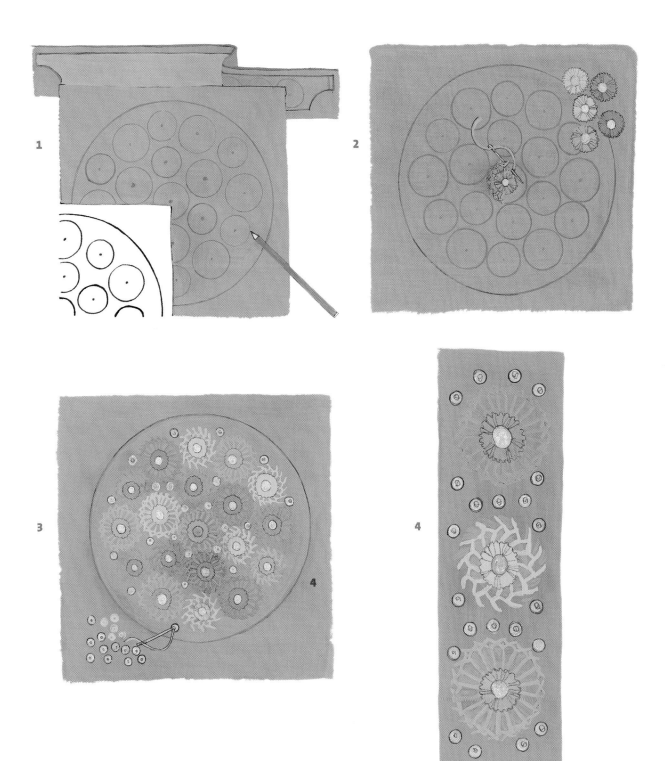

1

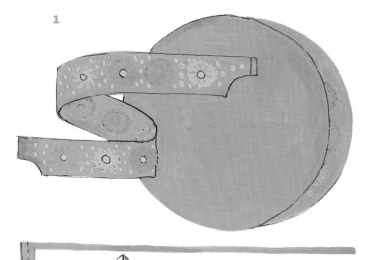

2

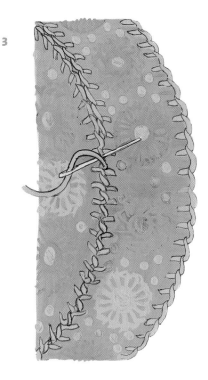

3

FINISHING THE HAT

1 Cut out the crown and the band to the correct sizes and cut the felt linings and interfacing for the band to the same sizes. Iron on the interfacing to the inside of the hat band. Sew it up along the back seam and press the seam allowances back over the interfacing.

2 Sew the lining band together in the same way and then place the two inside one another wrong sides together. Pin and baste. Pin and baste the crowns together and buttonhole stitch them all around the outside using all six strands of the lime thread. Buttonhole stitch the band in the same way with the same colour.

3 Place the crown and the band together and pin at intervals. Using the same colour thread, join the two by running stitches between the two outside threads of the buttonhole stitches.

Shisa-mirror belt alternative

This bright belt consists of two bands of felt in contrasting colours, decorated with shisha mirrors as before, but stitched with contrasting coloured threads, and tied with Prussia braid. Cut out two pieces of felt to the chosen length and width of the belt, and cut out a piece of iron-on interlining to match.

1 Mark the positions of the mirrors along the length of one felt strip, about 6cm (2½in) apart. Remove the centres from four of the mirrors and set aside. Embroider the mirrors in contrasting coloured threads, positioning one empty one at each end of the belt. Cut off the corners at each end and iron the interlining on the back of the other felt strip.

2 Pin and baste the layers together and buttonhole stitch all the way around in one contrasting coloured thread. Cut eyelet holes inside the empty surround at each end and match the holes in the interlined strip. Stitch the remaining surrounds to the backs of the eyelets. Knot two lengths of shiny Prussia braid through the eyelet holes for the ties.

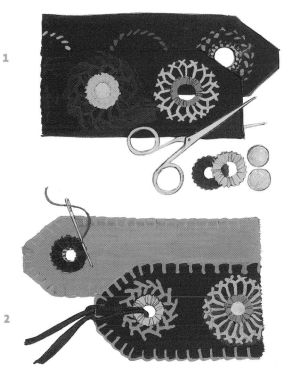

USEFUL INFORMATION

Basic embroidery techniques

Most of the projects in this book are very straightforward. You will, however, have to acquire a few basic design techniques (namely resizing designs and transferring these to your embroidery fabric – the designs and/or charts for some of the projects are given on pages 105–109) and a few stitching techniques (primarily how to stretch the ground fabric).

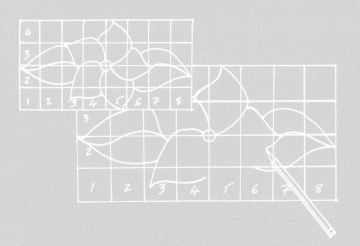

RESIZING DESIGNS

The most important decision to be made is the size of the design. Is it the correct size for your purpose? If not, the easiest way to change it is to use a photocopier either to reduce or enlarge it, but the traditional method for resizing is to square up the design onto a grid. Draw a grid over the initial tracing (using 1cm/½in squares); this is the usual size for small motifs. Decide how much bigger or smaller to make the design. Then draw another grid on a separate sheet of paper using the same number of squares but resized to fit the chosen dimensions; here the squares have been enlarged by 50 per cent. Transpose the drawing by matching the lines square by square.

TRANSFERRING DESIGNS

The next decision to make is the method to use to transfer the design to the ground fabric. The choice depends on the fabric and the type of design.

Light fabric method

If the fabric is transparent or very light in colour it is easy to lay the fabric over the tracing. Secure it with pins and then draw over it using a water-soluble pen. If you attach the fabric to a light source (such as a window pane), you can see through slightly thicker fabrics.

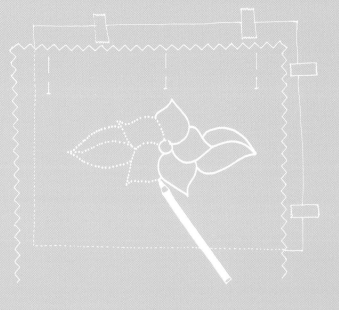

Carbon paper method

When the fabric is thick and opaque, the transferring system using dressmaker's carbon paper is the best one to opt for. Place the fabric on a hard surface and put a sheet of the carbon paper, colour side down, on top of it. Secure the tracing of the design in position using a few pins and then trace over the lines with a ball-point pen or a very sharp pencil. Use a colour that contrasts with the ground fabric but one that is not too dark as it may take a few washes to get rid of the chalk mark.

Transfer paper method

If the design is symmetrical (in other words, if the mirror image is identical to it), then you can use special transfer papers. All you have to do is to draw the design straight onto tracing paper using special transfer paper (fig 1), which can then be turned over so that the marked side is placed next to the fabric, pinned in position and then pressed with a cool iron (fig 2). The drawing transfers onto the fabric with the heat of the iron and washes out when the embroidery is complete.

1

2

PREPARING TO STITCH

When working embroideries on fine or soft fabrics it is advisable to stretch them prior to working on them, even if they are backed with another fabric for stability. Stretching ensures that the fabric lies flat after embroidery and does not pucker, shrink or distort owing to the tension exerted by the constant pulling of the stitches through the fabric. The design must be transferred onto the fabric first by any of the methods on pages 88 and 89; then, depending on the size of the motif, either a round hoop or a rectangular frame stretcher is used.

Working with a hoop stretcher

Hoop stretchers come in a variety of sizes, from very tiny ones to large quilting hoops. They are made of two wooden rings, with a screw adjuster. The fabric is slipped over the inner loop, and the outer hoop laid over the fabric, which is then stretched taut by adjusting the screws. They are easy to use as the work can be slipped off the hoop by just loosening the screw on the outer ring.

To ensure precise stitch placement, when working with the hoop the fabric must be stretched as tightly as possible without distorting the motif – it should ping when you flick it with your fingers. If you are right-handed, always work with the screw to the top left of the hoop (fig 1); if you are left-handed, then it should be on the top right. This saves the thread from catching on the tightening device.

It is advisable when stretching fine or slippery fabrics, satin or lightweight silks, to wrap the under ring with a length of soft muslin or fine cotton (fig 2). This both protects the delicate fabrics from the harsh wooden surface and also ensures a tighter grip. If very delicate fabrics are used then you can also wrap the outer ring in the same manner, securing the ends with a few tacking stitches to stop the cloth unravelling.

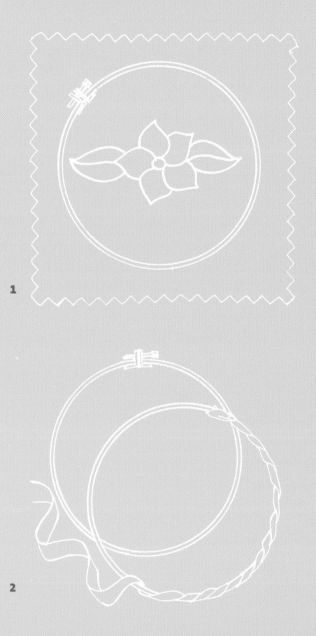

1

2

Working with a straight frame stretcher

A straight frame stretcher is useful for larger items and fabrics that would mark if a hoop were placed on to them – velvet, for example, would mark and require steaming to correct, and the threads of very fine gauze would distort and be ruined if placed on a round stretcher. Like the round frames, they come in various sizes up to 1m (1yd) in length. The most versatile stretchers are those with rollers as the horizontal bars, as the fabric can be rolled around the top and bottom bars so that only a small amount of the surface is exposed at one time.

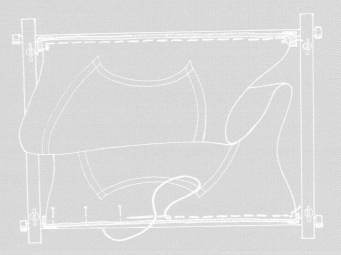

Stretching fabric on a frame

The ends of the fabric are first pinned and then basted to the strips of fabric tape attached to the top and bottom bars of the frame. The tension is applied by rolling the fabric so that the surface is evenly stretched top and bottom and the area to be embroidered is revealed. Further tension is ensured by sewing the fabric to the vertical bars at each side (fig 1). These stitches will need to be removed when another section of the embroidery is to be rolled on to be worked, and the process then repeated. An extra strip of fabric can be basted over the base of the work to protect it from getting dirty (fig 2).

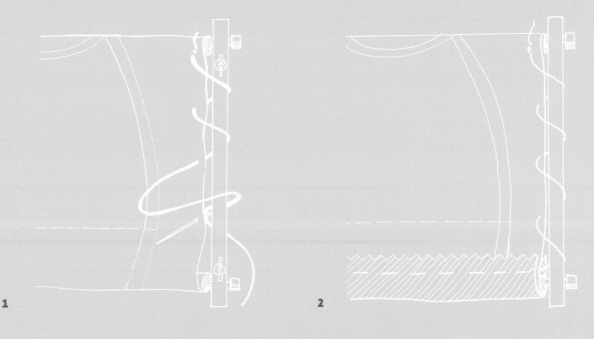

1

2

Stitch glossary

Learning to embroider is like any other skill: it requires a little practice to master it, but unlike many other crafts, it is easy enough for a child to do, as you can see from the many excellent stitch samplers that children as young as seven or eight years old produced in days gone by.

I have concentrated on basic stitches in this book, with one or two special ones for specific purposes. As in any other crafts, keen embroiderers often create their own working methods, and there is nothing to prevent you from working the stitches in a way that suits you best. There is a great deal of satisfaction to be had in achieving sufficient manual dexterity and control to produce stitches of a similar weight and length, and it is just this regularity which will give your work its desired elegance and appeal.

The different threads you use will make a great deal of difference to the effect produced by the stitches. Space-dyed yarns can be used to produce finely graded colour effects. Choosing the right stitch and appropriate thread for the purpose is a key element in achieving a professional finish.

RUNNING STITCH

The simplest stitch in a group known as straight stitches, running stitch simply involves taking the needle and thread in and out of the fabric in a line. It can be used to outline a motif, or to fill a design, and is one of the most frequently used stitches in quilting. Darning stitch is a variation on this stitch.

If you are right-handed, running stitch is worked from right to left. You need to create a rhythm that allows you to weave the needle in and out easily and with regular spaces between the stitches. Normally you would take two to three stitches a time on the needle before pulling the thread through, but on thick fabrics (for example when quilting) you may have to stab the needle through the layers of fabric, picking up only one stitch each time (this is known then as stab stitch).

CROSS STITCH

Also known also as sampler stitch or Berlin stitch, cross stitch
is internationally popular, and is found on traditional
embroideries in countries as far apart as Greece, Scandinavia
and India. A geometric stitch in the straight stitch family, it is
worked on evenweave fabric, which enables you to produce
perfectly even stitches by counting threads. Using waste canvas
allows you to create even cross stitches on other fabrics. There
are many variations of this stitch, but basic cross stitch is both
effective and popular.

Cross-stitch patterning can be achieved by various methods,
either line by line or by each single stitch made separately.
When shaped areas of design are to be covered, such as a letter,
it is advisable to work the technique in rows and count each
row as you go. This method also helps to achieve the correct
positioning of the topmost crossed stitch, so that it faces in the
same direction as all the others in the embroidery, which adds
greatly to the overall quality of the finished work.

BACKSTITCH

If you use a sewing machine, you will be familiar with this
stitch as the basic machine stitch. One of a group of straight
stitches, it creates a line of stitches with no space between
them, looking rather like a drawn line. To create similarly sized
even backstitches requires a little practice, so try out the stitch,
both on straight lines and curves, to perfect your technique.
The stitches are worked so that the needle is taken back to the
finishing point of the first stitch, to create an apparently
continuous line.
(Note: In the tufting variation used in the candlewick
technique, the backstitches are spaced slightly apart and the
thread is left looped rather than being pulled taut.)

SPLIT STITCH

Looking like a tiny chain stitch, split stitch is a variation of
backstitch as it is worked in the same manner, except that the
needle goes through the preceding stitch.

SATIN STITCH

One of the most widely used stitches in embroidery, satin stitch is used most frequently as a filling stitch. Made up of straight stitches worked close together in parallel lines, it is particularly useful for monograms, where it is padded to raise the stitch from the ground fabric and give the motif a 3D effect. The length of the stitches varies – short stitches at the point of a leaf and wider stitches towards the base – but very long stitches need to be avoided as they look untidy and can catch. Normally when filling a motif you make the shortest stitches first, working in parallel lines. To ensure an even outline, it pays to work the outline first in backstitch.

In order to create really even stitches, you will need to stretch the ground fabric in an embroidery hoop or frame.

STEM STITCH

This linear form of satin stitch, known as stem stitch, is worked as a series of short, straight diagonal stitches placed close to one another to form a continuous line.

FRENCH KNOT

These little jewel-like stitches are created by winding the yarn around the needle in the course of making the stitch, so that each stitch resembles a small bead. They are useful for creating textural effects. The number of times you wrap the thread around the needle increases the size of the knot. An embroidery hoop is useful for keeping the ground fabric taut. Practice will help to create neat, even knots.

BULLION KNOT

For this elongated version of the French knot, use a firm thread and a thick needle so that the thread can pass easily through the coils, which must not be allowed to slip out of place as they are pulled into the reverse position to anchor the stitch.

BUTTONHOLE AND BLANKET STITCH

One of the most popular and most useful of looped stitches, buttonhole stitch (fig 1) and its close cousin, blanket stitch (fig 2), are worked in exactly the same way, but in buttonhole stitch, the stitches are placed close together to form a single line of stitches, whereas in blanket stitch they are positioned a short distance apart. Both stitches are used to finish off raw edges and prevent them from fraying. As with all embroidery stitches, even, neat stitches are essential for a professional finish. To stitch a corner in blanket stitch, it is advisable to work an extra stitch on a slant into the corner as shown (fig 2).

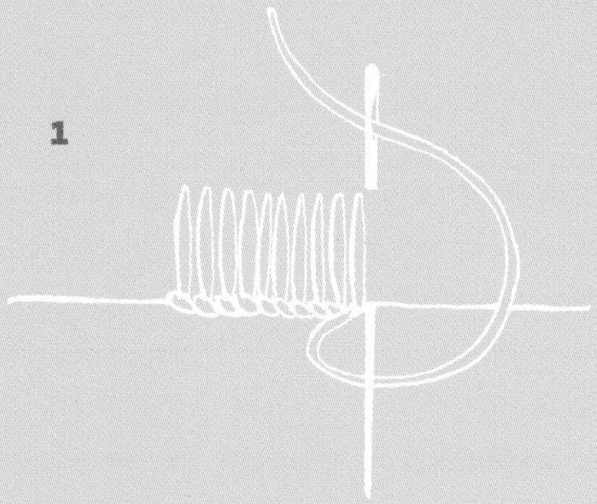

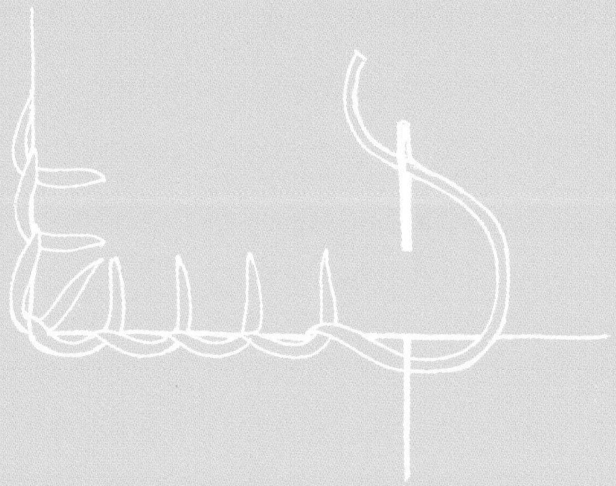

DECORATIVE BLANKET STITCHES

Decorative versions of blanket stitch are useful for edging cushions and throws. A closed blanket stitch variation forms neat triangles and gives a very crisp finish (fig 3). A circular blanket stitch variation (fig 4) is useful for florets and in traditional smocking embroidery.

DETACHED CHAIN STITCH

Chain stitch is a looped stitch (known as tambour stitch in the East where it worked with a fine hook). It is used primarily as an outline stitch but can also be worked close together in fine thread to make filling stitches. In the variation shown here (known as detached chain, or lazy daisy stitch when worked in a circle) the thread is looped under the point of the needle to make an extra small straight stitch, before the needle is inserted back into the ground fabric to create the next chain stitch.

1

2

3

4

HERRINGBONE STITCH

A traditional stitch in the cross-stitch family, herringbone stitch comes with many pseudonyms, as it is practised in many parts of the world. The slanting, crossed stitches are useful for joining fabrics together and prevent edges from fraying. They can be worked in many different ways to subtly alter the formation, so that in some versions the top of the row of herringbone stitches is more widely spaced to create a lattice effect. Its geometric look demands precision, so practise first to ensure your stitches are evenly worked.

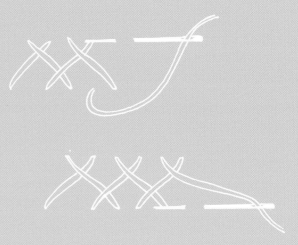

Variations

There are many additional stitches that can be made to the crossed sections of herringbone stitch to produce some highly decorative and very elegant lines of embroidery.

The extra stitches can be made in different coloured threads to the basic herringbone line.

1 Running stitches are placed over the two sets of crossed stitches. Sew one line at a time.

2 Straight stitches are sewn vertically over the crosses. These can be stitched in a single row at a time by alternating the upper and lower stitches.

3 The combination of theses two stitches, running and straight, makes a cross-stitch variation.

4 Single chain stitches decorate the herringbone line. These can be repeated on the upper line of crosses for a very decorative effect.

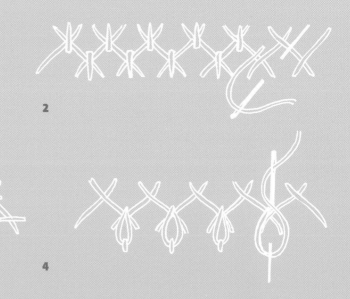

1

2

3

4

FEATHER STITCH

Belonging to the group of looped stitches, feather stitch was widely used for smocking. Similar to blanket stitch, but with the arm of each stitch placed at an angle instead of vertically, the stitches are worked on either side of a central line to create an open "feathery" appearance. It is particularly useful for covering raw edges and as such is often used in crazy patchwork to cover the joins between the pieces.

Variations

1 Single feather is a slanting buttonhole stitch worked along a straight line.

2 Double feather has an added number of looped stitches to extend the diagonal line to make a pronounced zigzag effect.

3 Cretan stitch is a straight-stitched feather stitch variation which can be used to decoratively cover seams in patchwork.

4 & 5 Variations of feather stitch used to fasten shisha mirrors to the ground fabric.

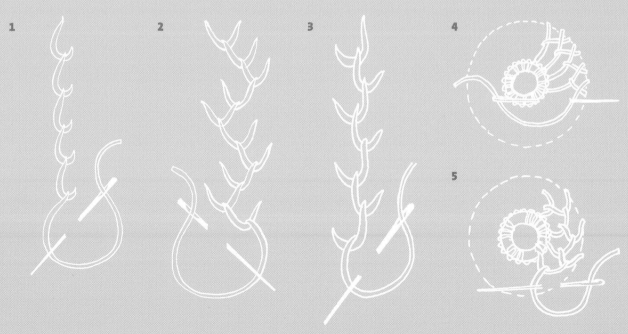

STAR STITCH

This pretty stitch is really a group of four large straight stitches that are criss-crossed and then tied down with a smaller cross stitch at the centre. It is very pretty when used to powder the surface of a fabric either in an even pattern or randomly spaced. More often it is used in conjunction with other stitches to augment a design or as a centre for flowers, or as a circular motif.

THORN STITCH

The name of this stitch is apposite – it looks exactly like a twig with straight thorns sticking out from it. It is really a form of couching (where stitches hold a thread in place), as the long straight thread (fig 1) is held into position by the shorter angled threads (fig 2). The variation (fig 3) is worked with the shorter threads worked closer together so that leaf shapes can be made with it. By varying the lengths of the slanting stitches many other undulating linear patterns can be made.

1

2

LANE OR LAZY BEADING

This quick method of beading is a form of couching as the beads are strung onto the secured thread (fig 1) and then couched down into position with a short stitch between the beads (fig 2). The couching threads can be used between every other bead if any undulations or curves need to be described, or between small numbers of beads for a quicker method.

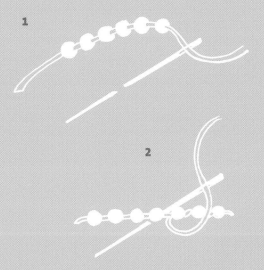

JACOBEAN LAID WORK

This filling pattern is a quick and easy way to cover a large area of fabric with embroidery. The technique is a couching one where the under threads are laid in long lines which criss-cross and in which they are held in place with a series of straight cross stitches.

To work the stitch, lay down a series of parallel threads over the whole area of the pattern to be covered,.taking care to measure the spaces between the lines accurately. Stitch another set of lines across the first set making a trellis (fig 1).

Work a series of cross stitches over the joins of the trellised threads (fig 2); this secures the whole embroidery into position. It is generally neater and quicker to work the cross stitches in separate rows almost like running stitches, rather than working each stitch individually, this method also ensures that all the top crossed stitches are worked in the same direction, which adds to the fluency of the embroidery.

INSERTION STITCHES

There is a range of useful stitches for drawn-thread work. I use just some of them, which are shown below:

Double border hem stitch

This is really herringbone stitch worked as a drawn-thread stitch. It has many other names, such as herringbone insertion stitch. It is worked over a line of woven fabric which is left intact when the threads have been withdrawn from both sides of the stitches, leaving a narrow band of solid fabric. The rows of withdrawn threads are divided into groups which are stitched together in alternating pairs, either side of the lines of horizontal threads, and a new section of threads picked up with each stitch, to form a decorative and lacy design.

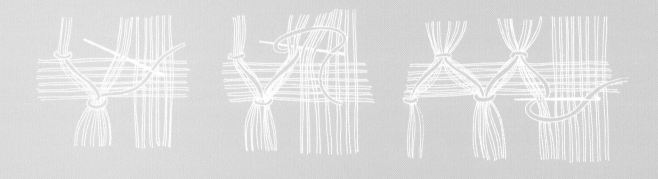

Coral knot insertion stitch

This simple knotted stitch is usually worked as a decorative line but it is used as an insertion stitch to tie together an even-numbered groups of threads, to keep them firmly in position in a channel of withdrawn threads. Here, groups of threads are drawn together with a line of coral stitches and the threads are stitched together in clusters of six. This stitch looks neat when viewed from the back so it is ideal for a scarf, for example, where the reverse side is often on view.

Twisted insertion stitch

The common name for this stitch is faggoting and it is used to join two separate pieces of braid or of hemmed fabrics together, so that a space remains between them. The pretty looped stitch shows clearly between the joins. Use a firm thread and keep an even space between the two edges of fabric being stitched together.

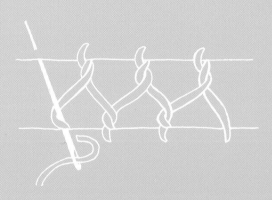

Making up

While many of the projects can be embroidered on found objects, here are the making up instructions for those you may want to create yourself, in order to have the greatest choice of fabrics or shapes.

BEADED BAG

The little beaded evening bag (see page 32) has an embroidered front and handsewn edges.

Using the pattern-piece shape on page 106, cut out the embroidered fabric, leaving the correct seam allowances as marked. Using the same pattern, cut out a piece of lightweight fusible wadding and the lining. Press the wadding onto the back of the embroidery (fig 1). Place the embroidery and the lining right sides together, pin and baste them, then machine stitch them together all the way around leaving a small 5cm (2in) gap in the side of the bag (fig 2). Turn right side out through the gap left in the side and lightly press all the seams on the lining side. Slip stitch the gap to close. Fold the bag in half, right sides together, and stitch the sides up through the machine stitches, from the fold to the top, leaving a 3cm (1½in) slit (fig 3). Finally, oversew the rings of the handle onto the small shoulders of the bag using a matching thread (fig 4).

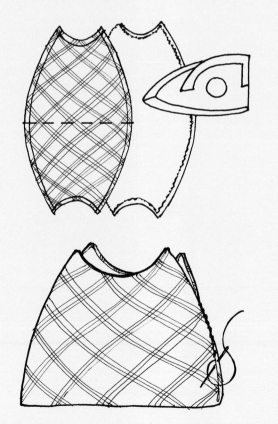

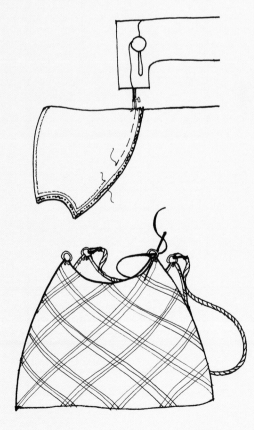

PICTURE FRAME

The instructions here are for the picture frames on pages 56–61. You can find ready-made card frames that you can cover with your embroidery. Here are the instructions:

Place the frame on a piece of wadding, and cut the wadding to the exact size of the frame (fig 1). Using fabric glue, fix it into position. Leave to dry.

Place the cardboard frame (made initially to measure the embroidery) onto the back of the finished embroidery and mark around the outer edge of it with a water-soluble pen or silver marking pencil. Cut a cross at the centre of the frame, taking the cuts as far into the corners as you dare without cutting any of the beaded embroidery while doing so (fig 2).

Place the frame, padded side down, on the back of the fabric again. Apply glue to the inside edge and pull the fabric through the hole into position. Make sure that the all the fabrics are securely caught in position (fig 3).

Pull the outside edges of the fabric onto the back of the frame and glue these(fig 4). You may need to trim them slightly first to neaten. Start with the top and bottom first and make sure that these are even by checking that no pen marks appear on the front. When these two sides are secured, pull the side pieces to the back and glue them. The frame is ready to be assembled according to the manufacturer's instructions.

1

2

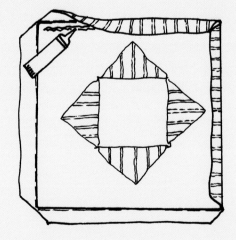

3

4

CUSHION COVERS

There are two methods of making up a cushion. The instructions for Version 1 are suitable for the flame-stitch cushion on pages 70-71. Those for Version 2 are suited to the bull's-eye cushion on pages 24–29.

Version 1

Sizes for the canvas front and two fabric back pieces (including a 2cm/¾in seam allowance all around) are given in the instructions.

Make a 2cm (¾in) hem on the centre of each back piece (fig 1). Overlap the two back pieces and place them RIGHT sides together with the embroidered canvas. Pin and baste all the way around and machine stitch (fig 2). Trim off the corners close to the stitching line and turn right side out. The cushion pad is inserted through the split, without the need for further fastenings.

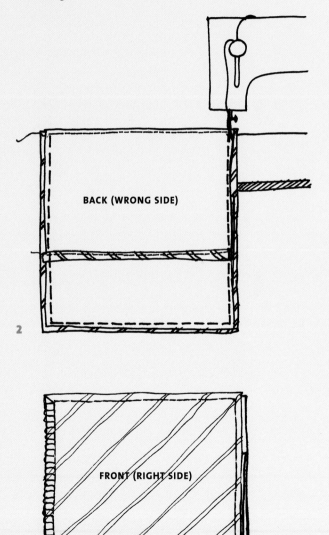

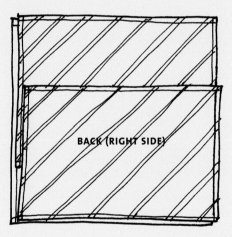

1

2

Version 2

There is no need to hem the front and two back pieces as felt does not fray. Draw a stitching guideline 1cm (½in) from the edge in water-soluble pen all the way around the appliquéd front. Pin and baste the WRONG sides of the front and back together, overlapping the back pieces. Carefully machine stitch over the guideline using monofilament thread. On the cushion front, blanket stitch the edges in your chosen buttonhole variation (see page 95) using the machine line as a guide to the length of the stitch (fig 3). Blanket stitch the edge of the uppermost back piece as well.

3

CANDLEWICK BOLSTER

The instructions here are for the bolster shown on pages 50–55; it measures 25cm (10in) in diameter by 90cm (36in) in length.

Cut one central piece of fabric 81 x 97cm (32½ x 37in) with the stripes running parallel to the shorter sides. Cut two end pieces 81 x 16cm (32½ x 6½in) with the stripes running parallel to the shorter sides. When the embroidery is completed, stitch the ends to the central piece and press open the seams (fig 1).

Fold the fabric in half along the length and pin and baste the seam. Machine stitch the seam but leave a hole through which to thread the gathering cord by double stitching the first 2cm (¾in), then leaving a gap of 1cm (½in) before continuing to the end, where the same size gap and double stitching are repeated (fig 2).

At each end of the bolster, turn under 5mm (¼in) and press into position, then machine stitch. Turn under another 1cm (½in) hem, large enough to accommodate your cord, and pin and baste in place. Machine stitch around the whole circumference of the cushion (fig 3) and turn right sides out. Thread the cord through the holes that are left in the inside of the channel.

1

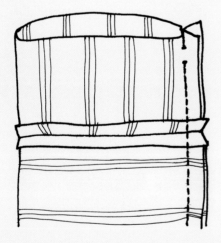

2

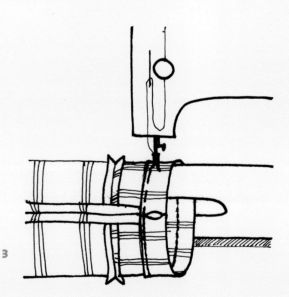

3

CRAZY PATCHWORK BOOK COVER

The instructions for the book cover shown on pages 36–39 are for a standard cover for an A4-size folder or book.

Trim and hem the narrow sides of the embroidery cover with a double-folded machined hem or a single one that is decoratively buttonhole stitched. Place the embroidered side of the fabric face down and lay the open book on top of it. Fold the ends of the fabric over the open book cover and mark the fold line and top and bottom of the book with a water-soluble pen on the inside of the fabric (fig 1). For a fatter book, fold over the fabric with the book closed, and mark the positions (fig 2).

Press the folds and then fold the fabric to the opposite side so that the right sides are together. Machine or backstitch these short seams in position, and snip off the corners close to the stitching (fig 3).

Turn the cover right side out. Fold under and press the top and bottom edges into position and trim any excess fabric away if necessary. Herringbone stitch (see page 96) in place, taking care not to stitch right through to the front of the embroidery (fig 4).

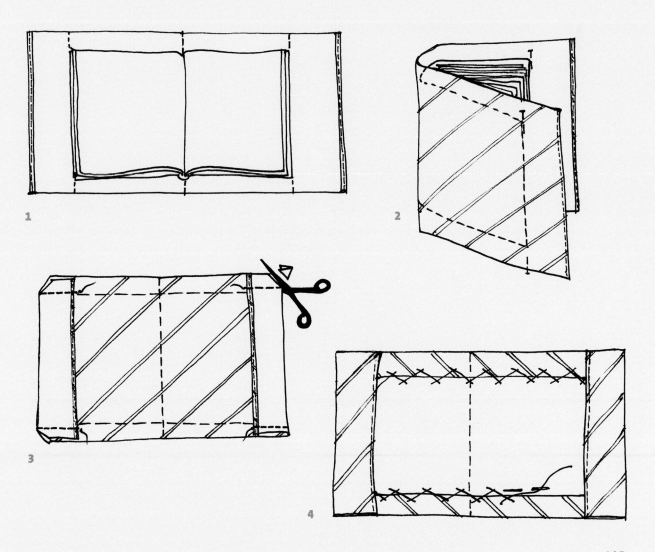

1

2

3

4

Motifs and charts

The charts and motifs required for the projects are shown on the pages that follow. Check the information with each motif to work out the actual sizing.

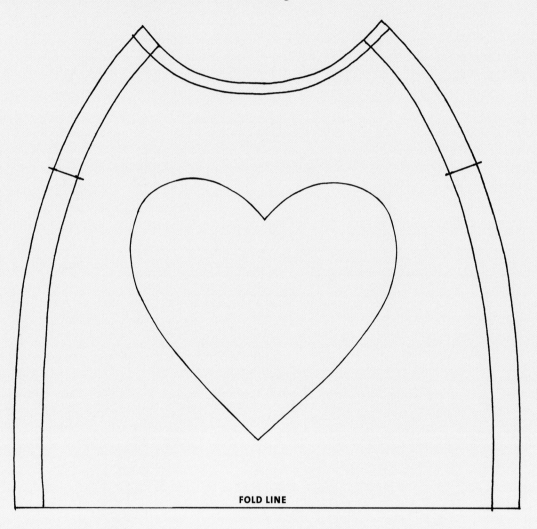

FOLD LINE

BEADED EVENING BAG
(see pages 30–35)
To achieve the actual size for the bag, enlarge the outline above by 70 per cent (ignore the heart). Lay the bottom edge on a fold of fabric (to make a joined front and back).

HEART APPLIQUE QUILT
(see pages 40–45)
Use the heart motif above for the hearts on the appliqué quilt. For the actual size, enlarge by 100 per cent.

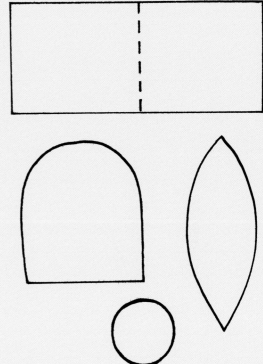

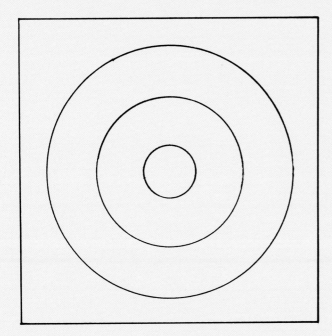

FELT FLOWER BAG

(see pages 74–79)

The diagrams above show the pattern pieces for this design. Enlarge the overall diagram (above left) by 330 per cent. The pieces for the individual flowers (above) are actual size.

BULL'S-EYE CUSHION

(see pages 24–29)

The diagrams left are those for the four individual patch pieces for this cushion. For the actual size, enlarge by 46 per cent.

FLAME-STITCH CUSHION

(see pages 68–71)

Transfer this design to graph paper; each stitch covering 7 squares of graph paper. Enlarge it by 360 per cent to achieve actual size.

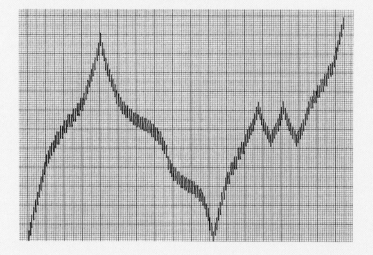

MEXICAN-STYLE ESPADRILLES

(see pages 18–23)

You will need a left- and right-foot design for the pair of slippers. The design is shown here actual size.

TRADITIONAL FLORAL MOTIF

(see pages 62–7)

Enlarge the rose design above by 170 per cent for the size of the project.

SHISHA-MIRROR HAT

(see pages 80–85)

The hat top pattern is shown below; the hat band pattern (right) represents half of hat band. Place the straight short edge on the fold of the fabric (to make double length). Enlarge the hat top and band by 87 per cent for actual size.

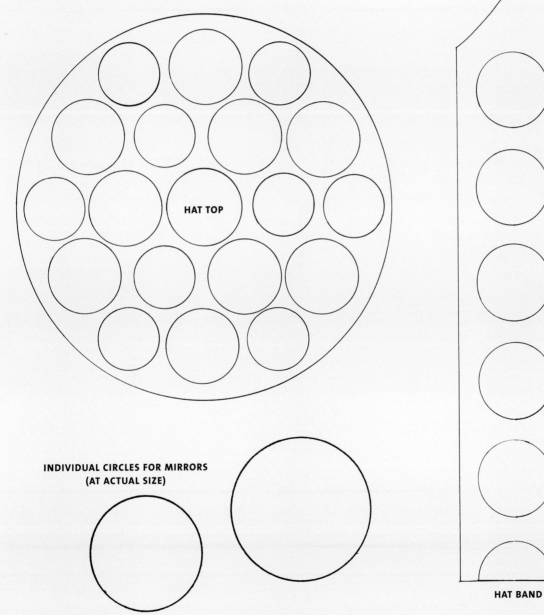

HAT TOP

INDIVIDUAL CIRCLES FOR MIRRORS
(AT ACTUAL SIZE)

HAT BAND

Project profiles

The photographs below showcase the principal projects in this book. Some are available as kits from Coats Crafts UK (see Suppliers, opposite). You can find further information about them, and about similar projects and kits from the sister volume to this book, on the Coats Crafts website.

Mexican-style espadrilles, p. 20

Bull's-eye cushion, p. 26

Beaded evening bag, p. 32

Crazy patchwork book cover, p. 38

Appliqué quilt, p. 42

French knot scarf, p. 48

Candlewick bolster, p. 52

Running-stitch frames, p. 58

Traditional floral motif, p. 64

Flame-stitch cushion, p. 70

Felt-flower bag, p. 76

Shisha-mirror hat, p. 82

SUPPLIERS

Almost all the products featured in this book can be obtained from Coats Crafts UK. In addition to the range of Anchor threads, they also stock all kinds of embroidery equipment, from needles and pins to hoops and frames, together with designing equipment, such as water-soluble pens and different tracing papers, plus a good range of embellishments, such as shisha mirrors, beads, sequins and braids, as well as special embroidery grounds and a selection of fabrics.

For further information, visit the Coats website (www.coatscrafts.co.uk) or get in touch with them at:

Coats Crafts UK
Lingfield House
McMullen Way
Darlington
Co. Durham, DL1 1YQ
Tel: +44 (0) 1325 394394

Knitting yarns used in this book, together with some patchwork fabrics, are available from:

Rowan Yarns
Green Mill Lane
Holmfirth
West Yorkshire, HD9 2 DX
Tel: + 44 (0) 1484 681881
www.knitrowan.com

Overseas stockists

There are branches of Coats Crafts in most countries. The following are the principal website addresses, but if you wish to find others, check out the main website:

North America: www.coatsandclark.com
India: www.coatsindia.com
Germany:www.coatsgmbh.de/de/1/hme.html
Portugal:www.coatsclark.pt/pt/1/hme.html
Brazil: www.coatscorrente.com.br

Kits

Several of the projects shown in this book are available in kit form. To find out more about them, or about other kits, contact Coats Crafts at the above address or visit your local crafts stockist. (Details of stockists throughout the country are listed on the Coats Crafts website).

Additional suppliers:

Whaleys (Bradford) Ltd,
Harris Court, Great Horton, Bradford,
West Yorkshire. BD7 4EQ
email: whaleys@btinternet.com
website: www.whaleys.bradford.ltd.uk
Suppliers of all white and unbleached fabrics: cotton, linen, silk, wool, net and calico.

ACKNOWLEDGEMENTS

My thanks go to the many people who contributed to this book: to Susan Berry, my editor and collaborator, and Stephen Sheard, for providing the impetus for this venture;.to the marketing and liaison teams, under Donald McMillan at Coats in Darlington and under Kate Buller at Rowan Yarns in Holmfirth, who promptly supplied the many and varied products for the projects.

I am indebted also to Anne Wilson for her elegant design for the book, John Heseltine for his luminous photography and Sally Harding for her eye for detail on the text.

I am also indebted to my colleague, Hilary Jagger, who kept me and my business alive with her optimism and humour while making projects for the book. Also to Nigel Hurlstone, fellow embroiderer, who helped me to research several new techniques, and was discovered stitching the flame-stitch cushion between courses at a restaurant, to help meet an imminent photoshoot deadline! Katie Phythian, a BA (Hons) embroidery student, who gave me much needed help preparing materials and June Baker-Atkinson, who made props for photography. I am also indebted to Adrian Campbell for the image of the Anemones on pages 56 and 60 and to Roy Grange for the wire-haired fox terrier on pages 60 and 61. And last, to my husband, Stephen Jacobson, who kept me sane throughout .

Index

Index compiled by Marie Lorimer